For Rodelle

GENERAL
SHERMAN'S
Christmas

Smithsonian Books

An Imprint of HarperCollins*Publishers*

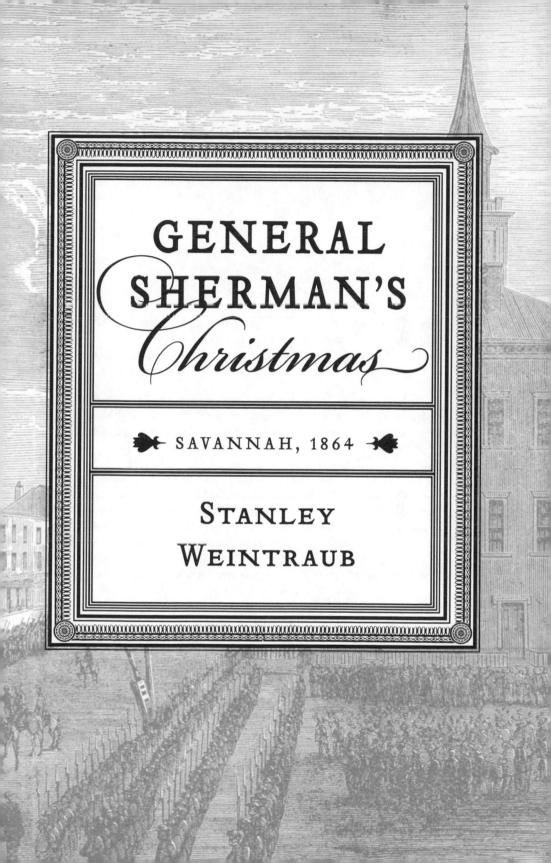

GENERAL SHERMAN'S *Christmas*

SAVANNAH, 1864

STANLEY WEINTRAUB

HarperCollins books may be purchased for educational, business, or
sales promotional use. For information, please write: Special Markets Department, HarperCollins Publishers, 10 East 53rd Street, New
York, NY 10022.

All illustrations are from 1864–1865 issues of *Harper's Weekly*, except:
page xvii, map titled "March to the Sea," is from *Marching Through
Georgia* by Lee Kennett. Copyright © 1995 by Lee Kennett. Reprinted
by permission of HarperCollins Publishers. Page 64, "Sherman's field
headquarters at dusk," and page 112, "Marching across a pontoon
bridge," *St. Nicholas Magazine*, 1864. Page 88, "Most shooting done
by Union troops"; page 101, "Soldiers wreck the imposing railroad
bridge"; and page 149, "General Foster greets Sherman," *Leslie's
Illustrated*, 1864–1865.

FIRST EDITION

Designed by Suet Y. Chong

Library of Congress Cataloging-in-Publication Data has been filed for.
ISBN: 978–0–06–170298–3

09 10 11 12 13 ov/qw 10 9 8 7 6 5 4 3 2 1

Savannah, Georgia, December 22, 1864

To His Excellency President Lincoln, Washington, D.C.

I beg to present you as a Christmas-gift the city of Savannah, with one hundred and fifty heavy guns and plenty of ammunition, also about twenty-five thousand bales of cotton.

W. T. Sherman,
Major-General

My Dear General Sherman,

Many, many thanks for your Christmas gift—the capture of Savannah.

When you were about to leave Atlanta for the Atlantic coast, I was <u>anxious</u>, if not fearful; but feeling that you were the better judge, and remembering that "nothing risked nothing gained," I did not interfere. Now, the undertaking being a success, the honor is all yours. . . .

Yours very truly,
A. Lincoln

CONTENTS

Unplanned and improvised, General Sherman's telegram offering President Lincoln "Savannah for Christmas" has been part of Civil War lore since Christmas Day in 1864. Yet much of the actuality of the event has slipped past history. How did the siege and capture happen? What was it really like, then and there? What hasn't, until now, been told? How much likely fiction in the multiplicity of accounts needs to be excised? The widely popular song of the year after, the jaunty "Marching Through Georgia," although boastfully accurate but for a single stanza, curiously opens with a misleading line in its first verse, and, even before that, a mistake:

> Bring the good old bugle, boys, we'll sing another song.
> Sing it with a spirit that will start the world along.
> Sing it as we used to sing it, 50,000 strong,
> While we were marching through Georgia.

No one sang the ballad while marching through Georgia. Although brass bands pumped "Blue Juniata" and the melancholy "When This Cruel War Is Over" to the patriotic "Rally Round the Flag" and the realistic "Tenting Tonight," Henry Clay Work, ironically named for a Southern senator, composed "Marching Through Georgia" the year after. Further, the soldier in the verse recalling the march would have known that General William Tecumseh Sherman's four army corps and independent cavalry brigade comprised over sixty—rather than fifty—thousand infantrymen and light artillery supported by several thousand horsemen.

Wreaking deliberate ruin, the three-hundred-mile march, familiar from many accounts, was a countrywide dose of noxious but needed medicine in a time of deadly plague. The civil war had been initiated in misguided idealism by Southerners claiming the right to detach their states from a union they felt was undermining lawful property rights to human beings. Northerners insisted that the federal union, once entered into, was indissoluble; and to keep it so, the war had become as inglorious as it was long. In its fourth year the idealism had vanished. Except for die-hards, the "glorious Cause" in the South was reduced to survival. The North had already paid a very high price for continuity. Although an attractive peace-and-compromise candidate was challenging President Lincoln's bid for reelection, the question was whether the disillusioned Union would settle for anything less than outright victory.

Unknown, little-known, and long-silent voices—from a semiliterate Illinois private and an unlettered Alabama farmer and his wife, to immigrant soldiers loyal to both North and South, and the nearly forgotten president's son who became a Rebel general—enrich this account of an episode that has belonged to myth as much as to history. However crucial, little significance has been given to the impact of Lincoln's once-doubtful reelection campaign, the first in which soldiers in the field cast ballots, upon whether the march from Atlanta would begin or would be aborted. Christmas in Savannah in 1864, and the future of the Union, might both have been very different had the "bayonet election" gone the other way.

Just before the drive to the sea began, a Georgia clergyman innocent of wartime wrongdoing penned a protest to Sherman that a horse to which he had title had been stolen by a Federal rifleman near Atlanta. Since looting and burning by both sides were the inevitable byproducts of war, Sherman deplored the theft but cautioned that "the great board of claims in Washington" would be useless in their lifetimes, or even "by the time your grand-child becomes a great grandfather." He had no immediate remedy. "Privately, I think it was a shabby thing in the scamp of the 31st Missouri who took your horse." Still, Sherman assured the clergyman that he could not repair the sins of the horse thief's superiors, although they were his own subordinates, even up to the brigadier level. "'When this cruel war is over,'" he wrote, echoing a wistful song sung by both sides, "and peace once more gives you a parish, I will promise, if near you, to procure out of one of Uncle Sam's corrals a beast that will replace the one taken from you so wrongfully, but now it is impossible. We have a big journey before us and need all we have, and, I fear, more too; so look out when the Yanks are about and hide your beasts, for my experience is that all soldiers are very careless in a search for title. I know that Gen. Hardee will confirm this, my advice."

William Hardee, the shrewd Georgia general whom Sherman would confront in Savannah, was also a realist about war, Sherman implied; yet the implacable Hardee, consumed by the Cause, would continue to fight a war already well lost. Sherman's "big journey" into the last Christmas of the war follows.

MID–NINETEENTH CENTURY WRITERS often capitalized words at random, and spelled with dismaying inaccuracy and inconsistency. Between quotation marks such variations are let stand. Among oft-used nouns (sometimes used as adjectives) both capitalized or left otherwise, and spelled in a variety of ways in singular and plural uses, are Negro/negro and Black/black. Again, these are printed as recorded, within quotations. Military ranks altered, usually upward, during the war. Often a writer will refer to a person by a later rank. These remain as written. Spoken dialogue, even from participants, often differs in details. Since memory sometimes slips, primacy is given to the person writing closest to the events. Proper names are sometimes at odds in different accounts. Here, later research is awarded primacy over recollection.

—Stanley Weintraub
Beech Hill
Newark, Delaware

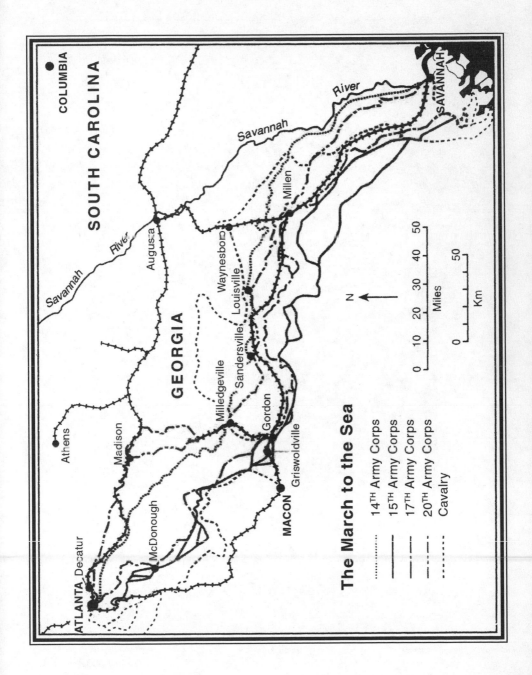

The March to the Sea

14ᵀᴴ Army Corps
15ᵀᴴ Army Corps
17ᵀᴴ Army Corps
20ᵀᴴ Army Corps
Cavalry

COLUMBIA

SOUTH CAROLINA

Savannah River

GEORGIA

Savannah River

Athens

Madison

Augusta

Waynesboro

Louisville

Sandersville

Milledgeville

Millen

SAVANNAH

McDonough

Gordon

Griswoldville

ATLANTA Decatur

MACON

N

0   10   20   30   40   50
        Miles

0   50
        Km

ONE

Voting with Their Feet

EW IN THE EMBATTLED UNION STATES EARLY in 1864 had Savannah on their minds. Rather, they wondered whether Abraham Lincoln should be nominated for a second term, let alone keep the White House. In the South, however, the *Savannah News* confidently expected to see "the North torn by internecine feuds, and utterly demoralized in the Presidential election." The results augured otherwise.

By Thanksgiving Day, November 24, newspapers from Confederate Richmond picked up in occupied towns and railway stations offered complete results of what was being described, because of its unique military dimension, as the "bayonet vote." Via the Rebel press, the news reached Major General William Tecumseh Sherman's troops pushing across Georgia toward Savannah. Preliminary tallies, including balloting by troops in the field, had been wired down soon after the polls closed. Unwilling to open what might be an aborted campaign if the opposition candidate had won, Sherman had awaited the certainty of Lincoln's reelection before ordering telegraph wires severed to insulate his army from both North and South.

Christmas Eve was a month away. Sherman planned to have his campaign completed by Christmas. The merry excesses of a plantation holiday were already diminished by the dark uncertainties of looming Southern defeat. Traditionally, approaching Christmas meant the festive firing of guns and their symbolic equivalent, firecrackers, alluded to by a younger Robert E. Lee when he wrote, wryly, to a recently married lady about her wedding night, "Did you go off well like a torpedo cracker on Christmas morning?" Now, as Confederate commander, the harassed Lee heard the crack of guns daily in Virginia and was unable to send any of his thinning gray line farther south to contain further Federal encroachments into Georgia.

En route eastward, Sherman's bluecoats would have to harvest their own festive Thanksgiving from "secesh" country. Although the holiday had originated in colonial Massachusetts in 1621, Lincoln had declared the feast of turkey and pumpkin pie a national observance in 1863, only the year before. Confederate president Jefferson Davis preempted what he could of the occasion the following year by proclaiming November 16, 1864, a day of prayer for divine guidance, "to restore peace to our beloved country, healing its bleeding wounds and securing to us the continued enjoyment of our right of self-government and independence."

As the Federals foraged their way eastward, the secession South, harassed and hungry, now had even less for which to be thankful, and the holiday was ignored where sweet potatoes, corn, and cotton grew. Bluecoats less remote from the North were beneficiaries of what Assistant Secretary of War Charles A. Dana, former managing editor of the *New York Tribune*, described as "the great turkey movement"—locally run campaigns to furnish "Thanksgiving boxes" for the army. On October 27, 1864, George W. Blunt, a Manhattan editor, had proposed that "something be done for the Army and Navy" for Thanksgiving, "not only to aid them in keeping the day properly, but to show them they are remembered at home." Blunt suggested sending the troops in blue "poultry and pies, or puddings, all cooked, ready for use," estimating that it would take 50,000 turkeys and a like number of pies, individually boxed, just to feed the 220,000 men in the Shenandoah Valley and stalled above Richmond, where Confederate war office clerk John B. Jones would note in his diary that their unmarked Thanksgiving, indulged in only by the enemy, was "like Sunday, with an occasional report of cannon down the river."

"George Bliss, Jr. of New York," Secretary Dana wrote, "telegraphed me, on November 16, 1864, that they had twenty thousand turkeys ready in that city to send to the front." He meant northern Virginia rather

EXODUS OF CONFEDERATES FROM ATLANTA

than inaccessible Georgia. Bliss, a prominent Republican attorney and a founder of the Union League, was then a colonel and paymaster general of the state militia. "From Philadelphia," Dana added, "I received a message requesting shipment to [Major General Philip] Sheridan's army of 'boxes containing four thousand turkeys, and Heaven knows what else, as a Thanksgiving dinner for the brave fellows.' And so it was from all over the country." It became Christmas in advance for Federal troops within railway reach—as Sherman's were not.

Sherman's divisions had spent the summer and early autumn destroying railway trackage in the lower Confederacy and marching farther and farther from Union territory. Moving south in midsummer from Tennessee into Georgia, he had managed to avoid costly confrontations until he reached the barrier of Kennesaw Mountain. Shrugging off three thousand casualties, he pushed on against General Joseph E. Johnston's outnumbered troops—"Johnnies," for *Johnny Reb,* to the bluecoats— reaching Peachtree Creek on the outskirts of Rebel Atlanta.

Replacing Johnston at Jeff Davis's order, the tenacious peg-legged John Bell Hood of Texas, who also had a crippled left arm, fought the Federals to a stalemate while the crumbling city and its dwindling inhabitants endured the hardships of a punishing siege that lasted all of August. Hard fighting was not to Sherman's taste. "Glory," he claimed, "was all moonshine; even success [at] the most brilliant is over dead and mangled bodies, with the anguish and lamentation of distant families." When possible he opted for evasion and maneuver.

With General Ulysses S. Grant stalled in Virginia short of Richmond after the failure of a costly, gruesome frontal attack on Lee's troops at the crossroads of Cold Harbor, the chances of Lincoln's reelection in November, even his renomination, seemed then diminished—until the besieged and battered Confederates evacuated indefensible Atlanta. When Grant had been summoned north as general-in-chief, Sherman, his closest deputy, emerged as top general from Tennessee southward. To

DESTRUCTION OF THE ATLANTA RAIL DEPOT
BY EXPLOSION AND FIRE

relieve the pressure on Grant's front opposite Lee, as well as to cripple Confederate capacity to continue the war, Sherman had plunged into Georgia. Atlanta seemed the communications and supply key to what remained of the South.

"So far as civil war is concerned," an Atlanta newspaper had downplayed early in 1861, after the first secessions, "we have no fears of that." Another cocky editor had prophesied that Southern women and children armed only with popguns firing "Connecticut wooden nutmegs" could cope with any Yankees in the unlikely event that they would materialize in Georgia. Although Hood had ordered the overloaded last Confederate ordnance train south, its eighty-one cars and five locomotives, with heavy artillery, supplies, equipment, and ammunition, were trapped once rail lines were cut. To keep the enormous prize from the Federals, the railway's buildings and rolling stock were torched, the contagion of explosion and flame outdoing Sherman's punishment. On the morning of September 2, Major General Henry W. Slocum's Union forces entered devastated Atlanta unopposed.

"A PRESIDENTIAL ELECTION then agitated the North," Sherman recalled sweepingly in his memoirs. "Mr. Lincoln represented the national cause, and [Major] General McClellan had accepted the nomination of the Democratic party, whose platform was that the war was a failure, and that it was better to allow the South to go free to establish a separate government, whose cornerstone should be slavery. Success to our arms at that instant was therefore a political necessity; and it was all-important that something in our interest should occur before the election in November."

Despite doubts about Lincoln after Grant's continued futility on the Richmond front, and the open efforts of party malcontents to replace the president, the Republican convention, reinventing itself as the National Union Party to embrace War Democrats, had renominated Lincoln. Andrew Johnson, a Tennessee Democrat, then its military governor, was put on the ticket to validate bipartisanship. No president since Jackson in 1832 had won a second term, and none since the mediocre Martin Van Buren had even been renominated.

With the outlook late in August still bleak, and General George McClellan the likely opponent, Lincoln penned a melancholy memo to be opened only after the election results were known. "It seems exceedingly probable that this Administration will not be re-elected," he predicted to his Cabinet. "Then it will be my duty to so co-operate with the President-elect, as to save the Union between the election and the inauguration, as he will have secured his election on such ground that he can not possibly save it afterwards." To guarantee its authenticity he asked each member to sign the back of the memo unread. (When the cabinet met on November 11, following the vote, Lincoln had his secretary, John Hay, unseal and read the slip, now moot.)

On August 29, 1864, enthusiastic pro-peace crowds had gathered in Chicago at the Wigwam, a sprawling convention center, to nominate the Democratic candidate, certain to be McClellan. Antiwar Democrats, the radicals who dominated the party, had been derisively christened "Copperheads" after the poisonous snake, a writer in the *Cincinnati Commercial* referring to the serpent in Genesis 3:14: "Upon thy belly shalt thou go, and dust shalt thou eat all the days of thy life." McClellan partisans shrewdly inverted the image, noting that Lady Liberty was portrayed on the "head" of the ubiquitous copper penny. Penny campaign buttons made by chopping the border from the coin promoted the liberty theme, which implied the freedom to continue slavery where jurisdictions wanted it.

Despite Copperhead concerns that McClellan would be unreliable as a peace candidate, delegates considered him their best bet to draw the soldier vote. To ensure the general's commitment, the convention would saddle him with a peace-at-any-price platform drafted by Clement Vallandigham's supporters, who saw the Union as beyond saving, and a running mate, George Pendleton, an Ohio Copperhead. Vallandigham, a former congressman from Ohio once jailed for his vocal defeatism, had been deported to the South. After slipping away to Canada, he had returned and moved about openly at the convention. While in Congress, his ally Pendleton had voted against all Federal war measures, from financing the army to conscription.

Long after the war, Jefferson Davis, recalling his feelings as he prepared for what would be the last session of the Confederate Congress on November 7, mused that the "peace party" Democrats, despite McClellan's Union loyalties, seemed an "encouraging" development—"and that the real issue to be decided in the Presidential election . . . was the continuance or cessation of the war." Downplaying the loss of Atlanta, he claimed that there were "no vital points [there] on the preservation of which the continued existence of the Confederacy depends. . . . Not the fall of Richmond, nor Wilmington, nor Charleston, nor Savannah, nor Mobile, nor of all combined, can save the enemy from the constant and exhaustive drain of blood and treasure which must continue until . . . the recognition of our indefeasible rights."

As reports of McClellan's nomination reached the Confederate lines in Virginia, loud cheers erupted and military bands thumped out Dixie songs. Defeat seemed stayed. Although Lincoln had been renominated, aspirants to replace him continued to surface, even from his own party. A divisive cabal of "Radical Republicans" had already met in Cleveland to nominate Brigadier General John C. Frémont, the "Pathfinder" of the West, as an alternative to Lincoln, with the idea that only a general could take bayonet ballots from the opposition. Yet two weeks after Atlanta fell, sensing his support draining, Frémont withdrew, claiming that his decision was "not to aid in the triumph of Mr. Lincoln, but to do my part toward preventing the election of the Democratic candidate." Still, he charged unhelpfully, much as McClellan had done in his cautious letter of acceptance, that Lincoln's presidency was "politically, militarily, and financially, a failure, and that its necessary continuance is a cause of regret for the country."

With misgivings, McClellan attempted to be a peace and war candidate at the same time. *Harper's Weekly* described his jockeying as requiring "an extraordinary exercise of the skill of the most accomplished equestrian simultaneously to ride two horses going different ways." Yet war weariness pervaded the North. New York political boss Thurlow Weed regarded Lincoln's reelection as "an impossibility. . . . The people are wild for Peace."

Although the president radiated renewed confidence as the strategic situation improved, he was running scared. Despite Atlanta, a humiliating defeat before Election Day might lose the soldier vote. Asked his opinion, Grant, who had a way with words, observed that "exercise of the right of suffrage by an army in the field has generally been considered dangerous to constitutional liberty, as well as subversive to military discipline. But our circumstances are novel and exceptional. A very large proportion of the legal voters of the United States are either under arms in the field, or in hospitals, or otherwise engaged in the military service. . . ." These were citizens of the several states performing a "sacred duty" which should not deny them "a most precious privilege." Soldiers had "as much right to demand that their votes shall be counted in their choice of their rulers, as those citizens who remain at home; nay more, for they have sacrificed more for their country."

It was not yet the practice for sitting presidents to campaign actively. Lincoln made only a few public appearances, usually to soldiers. "I happen, temporarily, to occupy this house," he told, with his characteristic humility, a regiment returning home. "I am a living witness that any one of your children may look to come here as my father's child has done. It is in order that each of you may have, through this free government which we have enjoyed, an open field and a fair chance for your industry, enterprise, and intelligence—that you may all have equal privileges in the race of life with all its desirable human aspirations—it is for this that the struggle should be maintained, that we may not lose our birthright. . . . The nation is worth fighting for to secure such an inestimable jewel."

Nineteen states initiated absentee ballots for troops, but mistrusting the way the bayonet vote might go, Democratic legislators in Indiana and Illinois blocked the process. As a result, a bluecoat unable to queue up at his campsite wrote unhappily on November 9, "Yesterday was election day; many soldiers [had] voted here, but we Illinoisans are disenfranchised." A Lincoln ploy had set up provisional state governments in partially occupied Tennessee, Louisiana, Arkansas, and Virginia, but radical Republicans in Congress excluded them from the electoral count. Reluctantly, the president gave in.

A foreshadowing of spared calamity for Lincoln came in early congressional elections on October 11 in Ohio, Indiana, and Pennsylvania. Republicans gained seats. "Treason has received a blow from which it may not recover," a relieved Indiana soldier wrote, "and traitors slink away into their holes where they will have time to consider their meanness, their worse than sinful course, and perhaps repent if repentance is for such vile creatures, which to my mind seems doubtful." William Robinson of the 34th Illinois wrote home anxiously that the choice "seems to be narrowed to that of Peace or war." William Bently of the 104th Ohio, "burning rails" in Georgia to deny trackage to the Rebels, wrote home that should McClellan win the presidency, "I shall almost despair of ever seeing our country restored to peace and happiness. If the Peace party prevails I shall be ashamed to own myself an American citizen."

Theodore Lyman, a colonel serving under Major General George G. Meade in the Army of the Potomac, wrote to his family that the early soldier vote seemed "unexpected" in its proportions, appearing "to show five to one for the Administration, . . . for troops in their private thoughts make the thrashing of the Rebs a matter of pride, as well as of patriotism." From the ranks a bluecoat explained that McClellan, his former commander, was not as disliked "as much as the company he keeps. There are a good many soldiers who would vote for McClellan but they cannot go to Vallandigham." Newly arrived in Georgia to be Sherman's military secretary was Major Henry Hitchcock, a St. Louis lawyer. In a letter to his wife on October 31, as soldiers voted early, he observed "that so far as I can learn by inquiry, and from conversation . . . , *one* in ten would be a large estimate of the McClellan men in the army. This is true even of the *New Jersey regiments*." (McClellan's home was in New Jersey.) Newspapers from the Confederacy filtered through the lines, giving Colonel Lyman the impression "that at no time during the war have the Rebel papers talked so desperately; they speak of the next month settling the question, and of arming the negroes. If they do this . . . , the slavery candle will burn at both ends. I have no idea that next month will settle it, though, of course, there is a chance for important movements during the autumn. . . ."

Southern newspapers had lost some of the feisty edge that had claimed superiority of character over the men who filled Sherman's ranks. In Columbus, Georgia, a prewar issue of the *Muscogee Herald* had derided the Northern "conglomeration of greasy mechanics, filthy operatives, small-fisted farmers, and moon-struck theorists . . . who do their own drudgery" as opposed to gallant Southern gentry who lived superior lives abetted by slave labor. Fortunately for Muscogee County, southwest of Atlanta, Sherman's conglomerate was turning eastward.

Preparing for the renewed march, in which he would be in Sherman's left wing, Brigadier General Alpheus Williams, commanding XX Corps, wrote to his daughter in Michigan on October 18 to explain his own ballot, contending that it would be "disgraceful" to abandon the war on Democratic Party terms: "I have no particularly strong personal reasons for loving the existing administration, nor do I, in everything, admire its policy or measures. Still, its great aim, in the emergency which absolves small things, is right."

An engraving for *Harper's Weekly* portrays soldiers in the field, shaded by several tall trees, lining up quietly to vote, with tents and covered supply wagons in the background. At a trestle table covered by a large American flag, a soldier sits on a packing crate inscribing his state ballot while officials opposite on other ammunition boxes witness the exercise of a citizen's franchise. Behind them, several senior officers, one in a folding camp chair, look on. How carefully such ballots were monitored for fraud, or multiple voting, was questioned by Democrats, but the system seemed sound. What happened in the states themselves, especially where corruption was common, did not trickle down to the field.

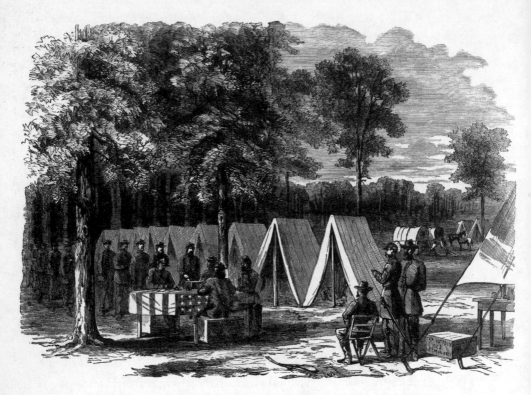

UNION SOLDIERS IN THE FIELD VOTING FOR PRESIDENT

A Michigan artilleryman wrote that the Copperheads would find it "better [to] be in hell" than in the hands of Union troops, but in New York City on November 2, where the former mayor, Fernando Wood, now a congressman, was a Copperhead, the Democratic-leaning *World* published a story only days before the election claiming that soldiers who had already balloted were overwhelmingly for McClellan, and that his election was "almost positive." As mayor in 1861, Wood had suggested to his city council that New York secede from the state and the Union in order to continue its profitable cotton trade from the South. From far upstate Watertown, where Major General "Fighting Joe" Hooker was taking tea with his brother-in-law, he told a cheering crowd from the portico in the aftermath of Atlanta that Sherman was "invincible" and set on preserving the Union. "The Union cannot be divided, let politicians talk as they may; for if division commences, where are you to end? First, the South would go, then the Pacific States, then New England, and I hear that one notorious politician has advocated that the City of New York should secede. . . . In such a case there would be no end to rebellion."

To the Copperhead *World*, the wicked Lincoln government was the "Black Republican Party" and the Emancipation Proclamation the "Miscegenation Proclamation." A political leaflet that could have been freely posted to troops, "Black Republican Prayer," sarcastically invoked divine blessing for the opportunity of every "sweet-scented Sambo" to "nestle in the bosom of every Abolition woman."

Wood had an ally in the new Democratic governor of New York, Horatio Seymour. To keep him from impeding the absentee service vote, his Secretary of State Chauncey Depew, a Republican, was charged by the state legislature with enabling soldiers to complete ballots to be sent to home districts by Election Day. Although New Yorkers were scattered by company and regiment all over the South, Secretary of War Edwin Stanton stubbornly refused to furnish their locations, arguing that it might aid the Confederacy. Yet the enemy must have known that New Yorkers were with Sheridan in the Shenandoah, and with Sherman in Georgia. They had fought, or were fighting still, from the Potomac to the Gulf of Mexico.

Intervening, Congressman Elihu Washburne of Illinois assured Depew, "You don't know Lincoln; he is as good a politician as he is a President, and if there is no other way to get these votes he would go round with a carpetbag and collect them himself." Implying what the outcome of a McClellan victory would be, Grant had written to Washburne, "The enemy are exceedingly anxious to hold out until after the Presidential election. Deserters come into our lines daily who tell us that the men are nearly universally tired of the war, and . . . they believe that peace will be negotiated after the fall elections." By the time that Depew arrived in Washington, the rigid Stanton had become the epitome of amiability. Depew returned by train that night with a list of every unit with New York troops, and their locations. When officials of local express companies considered on-time delivery of ballots impossible, Depew "sent for old Mr. [John] Butterfield, the originator [with Wells, Fargo] of the American Express Company, and stated the case to him. He said they were organized for such purposes, and if they could not accomplish them they had better disband. He then undertook to arrange through the various express companies, by his own direct superintendence, to secure the safe delivery in time to every company—and he succeeded."

Once Thurlow Weed told Lincoln that in the crews "on Gun Boats along the Mississippi" were "several thousand" New Yorkers who could vote only if absentee ballots reached them, the president authorized Secretary of the Navy Gideon Welles to put a steamer "at the disposal of the New York [election] commission." Welles also arranged for agents to visit naval facilities on land "for the purpose of receiving the sailors's votes," and also declared work stoppages in the yards on November 8, with "no muster," so that each civilian worker could "attend the polls and discharge his duty." Although there was no rigging of votes, Assistant Secretary Dana wrote, "All the power and influence of the War Department, then something enormous from the vast expenditures . . . of the war, was employed to secure the re-election of Mr. Lincoln. . . . There was a constant succession of telegrams from all parts of the country requesting that leave of absence be extended to this or that officer, in order that his district at home might have the benefit of his vote and political influence." Yet few in Sherman's regiments could be released unless they were to be culled from the march—and only the physically unfit, and a few senior officers with political clout at home, were furloughed. When asked, none knew where Sherman was going. Savannah for Christmas was only on a map in his saddlebags.

The Copperhead monthly *The Old Guard*, published in New York by a former Universalist minister, C. Chauncey Burr, wrote of Sherman's depredations en route to Atlanta, "We had no right to burn their wheatfields, steal their pianos, spoons or jewelry," and he declared that Lincoln should be tried "as Charles I of England was tried." Federal soldiers, Burr charged, were demoralized because the war to preserve the Union had become instead a war for emancipation of Negroes. It was "like a poison tainting the very fountain of life." Conscripts, he contended, would not support continuation of the conflict. A conspiracy by Democratic agents to procure fictitious and forged ballots, exposed in the *New York World* on November 1, 1864, failed. Depew's blank ballots for New Yorkers of any political persuasion were genuine.

McClellan's peace platform tempted some troops still in the line of fire, but Democrats promised only to end the war, not to attend to its causes. Skeptically, a soldier in Sherman's army wrote, "Then we can fight them again in ten years. But let old Abe settle it, and it is always settled." In Ohio, when soldiers broke up a Democratic rally, some Southern sympathizers saw the sporadic divisiveness as breeding opportunities to exploit, should casualties continue to mount as reported. The combatants already counted 656,000 dead from wounds and disease. The outmanned South would lose nearly twenty percent of its white men of military age. Hopefully, John B. Jones wrote from the Richmond war office, "This fire may spread, and relieve us."

About five hundred draft dodgers in Orange and Crawford counties in Indiana banded together to resist induction; in Clearfield and Cambria counties in Pennsylvania, over a thousand deserters and draft delinquents battled federal provost marshals, killing one before being broken up and jailed. Civil disorder in the North—there had already been serious draft riots, especially in New York City—might, if continued, force Lincoln to pull troops from the South. The border states seemed the most fragile. "McClellan seems to be in every body's mouth here and I don't think there will be any doubt about his being our next President. The old soldiers of the Potomac Army are nearly all for him," a soldier from southern Illinois wrote home. Yet the Army of the Potomac, badly outgeneraled for years, owed much of its exasperating seesaw situation inherited by Grant to the dithering leadership of his predecessors, McClellan included.

In reality, soldiers had enough of "little Mac." An Iowa soldier, John Rath, German-born and newly a citizen, wrote from his bivouac near Atlanta, "We participated in the election and I cast my first vote for Abraham Lincoln as President of the U.S." Henry Peck, a New York recruit, wrote home on learning how his family intended to cast its ballots. "I am glad to see that you are getting waked up to the necessity of all electing Uncle Abe by an overwhelming majority. If you at home will do your share you may rest assured that the soldiers are all right." Another New Yorker, John Gourlie, wrote to his brother about a soldier he knew who had once sworn he would "see Old Abe d—d before he would vote for him"—but that was before Gourlie had been captured and sent to a Rebel stockade. His guards there had boasted that McClellan would save the Confederacy. On escaping to Atlanta and rejoining his unit, the soured soldier had become a "Lincoln man to the backbone." Private John Brobst of Wisconsin wrote to his sister angrily about how his vote would go: "I could shoot one of them copperheads with a good heart as I could shoot a wolf. I would shoot my father if he was one." Soldier mail may well have influenced the election at home. Fully aware of the impact on morale in general, Sherman ordered trains still supplying the troops with food and munitions via Chattanooga and Nashville to make a priority of delivering the soldier post. Every evening, railway mail arrived, and at dawn departing trains hauled letters homeward.

Tom Taylor of Ohio, an officer and prewar lawyer, was politically torn. His brother-in-law, Chilton White, running for reelection to Congress on the Democratic ticket, had asked Taylor to campaign on his behalf among "the Boys of the 89th or 50th Ohio," as his Republican opponent was counting on the soldier vote. "McClellan is our *man* in this division," Taylor wrote supportively to his wife, Netta. "I never was, can, or will be a supporter of 'honest old Abe.'" Then he went home on leave, and on returning to his own regiment, the 47th Ohio, found he had been promoted to judge advocate on the staff of Major General William Hazen. "I won't have anything to do with any set of men opposed to this war," he now wrote to Netta. "My entire and radical change has been progressing during the last four years." Chilton White would lose—and Taylor, it turned out, would not even bother to vote. Although he "organized the election" in his regiment, he wrote in his diary on November 8, so few McClellan tickets showed up at Hazen's Second Division polling booth at Ruff's Station, north of Atlanta, that he felt it unnecessary to cast a ballot for "Father Abraham" himself.

George Trowbridge wrote to his wife, Lebbie, that he was "forsaking" the Democratic Party this time, and she responded, "Do you hold that the framers of the Chicago Platform that you so bitterly denounce are no longer [true] Democrats?" If "McClelland" were loyal to his country, she thought, agreeing with her husband, the general would have denounced them rather than run on their ticket. The congressional election results in the early-voting states had just come in. "Sherman's late victories"— she was referring to Atlanta—"and the voices of Pa Ohio & Indiana will, I should think, make the *copperheads* hunt for a hole in which to hide their deformed heads when the other states shall unite with these three next month, and speak in tones that will make traitors tremble." In the interim, soldiers worried about the impact of a military embarrassment. Even a small Rebel success, Captain Charles W. Wills wrote to his sister in Illinois, would have "political influence in the north. They know that their only hope is in the northern copperheads and they want to encourage them all they can about the time of [the] election."

On moving east, Sherman would attempt to suppress communications of every kind about the progress of his march from devastated Atlanta to the sea. Later, when he began to mention Savannah as his Christmas target, Sherman, a great reader, liked to quote a line from the Cockney innkeeper in Charles Dickens's *Barnaby Rudge*, set during the Revolution, whose son, wounded in Georgia, had taken the king's shilling: "Salwannis, where the war is."*

REPORTS ABOUT THE PRESIDENTIAL CAMPAIGN came to the Confederacy via the Washington press, which scoffed at Rebel hopes of an upset victory by the peace-and-appeasement McClellan. Sherman was amused by a letter from Washington from his brother John, an Ohio senator, that a paper claimed that the general had covertly pledged ninety-nine percent of his soldier vote to McClellan, whom he allegedly supported. "I never said such thing," Sherman assured his wife, Ellen. "I will vote for nobody because I am not entitled to vote." (He had not registered, which was typical of career officers.) "Of the two, . . . I would prefer Lincoln, though I know that McClellan, Vallandigham or even Jeff Davis if President of the U.S. would prosecute the war, and no one with more vigor than the latter." He thought that "the howl . . . raised against McClellan . . . was in a measure unjust, for he was charged with delinquencies that the American People are chargeable for."

Major Hitchcock was curious about Sherman's view, and after some probing, the General confided, "Now that we are alone, I'll tell you."

---

* Sherman had read the novel aboard the USS *Lexington* on a voyage from New York round the Cape to San Francisco in 1846, and would read, and reread, Dickens all his life.

McClellan had written to him twice, implicitly to solicit support, "and that has depreciated him more in my estimation than all else. He cannot be elected—Mr. Lincoln will be, but I hope it will be done quick, that voters [on leave to cast ballots in home districts] may come [back] to their regiments and not give the Rebs the advantage they know so well to take."

Always cynical about electoral politics, Sherman told Ellen that he had been receiving letters "to put me up for President," which was "cruel and unkind." He reminded her that when he had left the army to become, briefly and unrewardingly, a banker in post–Gold Rush San Francisco in the mid-1850s, he was solicited to run for state treasurer. "My answer was that I was ineligible because I had not graduated at the 'Penitentiary.' . . . I would receive a sentence to be hung and damned with infinitely more composure than to be the Executive of this nation."

A month and a day before Christmas it had become evident, even in the deep South, where news arrived late, that Lincoln had been convincingly reelected, and that the war would go on until the Confederacy had gone under. In South Carolina as late as November 17, Major General Mansfield Lovell, a Marylander who had lost New Orleans to the Union, after which he was given no new assignment and was sitting out the war, told Mary Chesnut, herself the wife of a general, "If Lincoln is not reelected, with his untold millions at command, his patronage, and his army and his navy, he must be a great fool indeed." On what was Thanksgiving Day for the Federals, Malinda Taylor, wife of an Alabama private, Grant Taylor, recruited from his farm, wrote disconsolately to him, "I suppose Lincoln is elected again but I dont know that makes it any worse for him to bee elected. Maybee him better than the other one. I disremember his name."

Until the last, Lincoln had worried that the charismatic McClellan, despite his failures against Lee, would preempt the soldier ballot. The Copperhead press had encouraged that perception. "We are as certain of two-thirds of that vote for General McClellan," the antiwar publisher Manton Marble prophesied confidently, "as that the sun shines." Recognizing that risk, Lincoln had encouraged the bayonet ballot, assuming little pacifism among bloodied troops. "I would rather be defeated with the soldier vote behind me," he told a White House visitor, "than to be elected without it."

Thirteen states had permitted in-the-field voting, and four others authorized proxy voting, with ballots in sealed envelopes returned for deposit in their districts. The legislatures of several states insisted that only those soldiers back home on Election Day could vote, prompting Lincoln to wire Sherman in Atlanta about his troops from Indiana, carefully noting it was "in no sense an order," and realizing that mass furloughs across contested areas were impractical, that "any thing you can safely do to let her soldiers, or any part of them, go home and vote . . . , will be greatly in point." Relinquishing Indiana "to those who will oppose the war in every possible way" might have "a bad effect upon the November election."

New Hampshire regiments on the Virginia front were informed that two official state commissioners, delegated by each major party, would be present on a fixed day in different sectors to oversee voting. "I was present," Major George A. Bruce of the 13th New Hampshire wrote, "and voted on that day. . . . Each man came up to the polling place and voted by himself. He was given two ballots, . . . and secretly, without knowledge of any one, he deposited whichever vote he saw fit. There had been no campaign literature circulated and no speechmaking. There probably never was a purer election held in the world."

Although absentee "bayonet" ballots were monitored for privacy as well as legitimacy, few in blue could keep their feelings to themselves. Both Republican and Democratic ballots were available, each participating state printing its own, including, named below the candidates, the Electoral College representatives who, constitutionally, did the actual voting. Soldiers chose a party ballot, and in the presence of an officer, or state designate, signed the back of the "ticket."

"Before leaving Atlanta," after "destroying all public property" in the city, Private Francis R. Baker of the 78th Ohio wrote in his diary, "we all cast our votes for President, and Lincoln received nearly the unanimous vote. This was my first vote for President—age 22." A letter from another soldier in Sherman's army, published in a Boston newspaper on November 4, before the general suspended all communications northward, offered preliminary and somewhat exaggerated statistics from Georgia that "nine-tenths of the soldiers . . . have voted for Lincoln. McClellan stood no sight whatsoever." Ballots tallied from tiny New Hampshire's soldiers gave Lincoln less of an edge—1,998 to McClellan's 679. In Maine the bayonet vote gave Lincoln 4,174, McClellan 738—a six-to-one margin.

Even in Camp Lawton, the bleak Confederate prisoner of war com-

THE PRISON PEN AT MILLEN

pound just above Millen in eastern Georgia, word had leaked in that November 8 was election day in the North. Lawton incarcerated 10,229 prisoners. Seven hundred would die of malnutrition, exposure, and disease before being moved from Sherman's expected path. The stockade, on the rail line halfway between Savannah and Augusta, had supplemented the notorious deathtrap of Andersonville, housing its overflow.* Since some prisoners knew of the soldier vote, Captain D. W. Vowles, the camp commander, hoped to make a political point by holding a mock election which he expected McClellan, the peace candidate, to win. The result was a landslide for Lincoln, which Vowles tried to conceal. Sergeant Lucius Barber of the 15th Illinois wrote in his POW diary, "A [symbolic] vote was taken in our detachment. There were two hundred twenty-four votes cast. Lincoln received one hundred eighty-eight and McClellan thirty-six. Over one-half of the men did not vote. Our rations continue very scarce. . . ."

ON ELECTION DAY, dark and rainy in Washington but brighter to the south, Sherman was headquartered in Kingston, northwest of Atlanta, close to railway trackage into Tennessee soon to be ripped up. Examining the 1860 census figures and large-scale maps for Georgia that he had requested from the Department of the Interior, he busied himself identifying from statistics on crop yields and livestock the counties that seemed prosperous enough to sustain a march of sixty thousand to the sea. (Admiringly, Grant had said of Sherman, "He bones all the time when he is awake, as much on horseback as in camp or in his quarters.") In one

---

* From mid-1864 to its end, Andersonville, where 30,000 bluecoats languished, received nearly 45,000 prisoners. The POW burial ground contains 13,714 graves. Its commander, Henry Wirz, charged with mass murder, was hanged in November 1865.

of his last telegrams north, Sherman asked the Navy to be prepared to receive him on the Atlantic coast. Gunboats offshore were to look for him just before Christmas between Savannah, the northernmost port in Georgia, and Hilton Head, just above the border in South Carolina.

Having boned up on Georgia farm production, Sherman informed Grant that the Federals could "stand a month's interruption to our communications." Since soldiers were to live off the land, as Sherman, to keep unnecessary supply trains from slowing them down, had sent surplus horse-drawn wagons north, "we received three crackers for five days' rations," Private Baker wrote jokingly. (Sherman's troops always marched with three days' rations.) A welcome bonus was included. "Before we broke camp to start on our march, a lot of captured plug tobacco was issued. There were three and a half plugs for each man, each plug about a foot long. So the tobacco users were well supplied, getting an extra ration from our comrades who had taken their portion but did not use it." It was almost like a premature Christmas.

Realizing the political consequences if the operation went awry, Sherman did not intend to break camp before the balloting. "The election is over," Major Thomas Osborn, of Major General O. O. Howard's staff, wrote to his brother, Abram Osborn, a minister in St. Louis, on November 10, from Smyrna, just north of Atlanta, "but we have not heard a word of the result. It will be a calamity if General McClellan is elected and becomes President with the copperhead party of the north at his back. However, I have no fear. . . . From present indications." Osborn closed cryptically, "I do not think you will hear from me again in a month or six weeks. I think we shall be cut off from mail facilities."

On her plantation east of Covington in Rebel Georgia, the widowed Dolly Lunt Burge wrote in her diary, "To-day will probably decide the fate of this confederacy[;] if Lincoln is reelected I think our fate is a hard one, but, we are in the hands of a merciful God & if He sees that we are in the wrong I trust that He will show it unto us. I have never felt that slavery was altogether right for it is abused by many. . . ." In the seasonal rhythm of the South, her slaves had already brought in the harvest, and some fattened livestock would not see another Christmas.

THE NEXT MORNING, early results were sent south by Major Thomas Eckert, supervisor of military telegraphs at the War Department. From Georgia, Tom Osborn wrote in a last letter to his wife, "From what we hear Lincoln must be elected as we have the report that all states so far as heard from have gone for him. McClellan's pro-slavery proclivities have ruined him, for providence had to go on with the great work and leave him behind." He did not think that McClellan had "a black heart," but had allied himself to the wrong sort. "It is now ten o'clock in the forenoon," Osborn wrote further to his brother Abram, "and the last train will pass here at twelve noon after which the railroad will be destroyed. After that," he added, going beyond metaphor, "we will be at sea from 300 to 500 miles from anywhere. I do not think you will hear from me again in less than six weeks. The Confederate newspapers will probably keep the country pretty well informed of our whereabouts and of what we are doing."

OF THE UNION ELIGIBLES, only Delaware and Kentucky, both emotionally "South"—and slaveholding—and New Jersey, McClellan's home state, went for the general. The soldier vote would make a political difference in Maryland, where the canvassing officer was required to wait "fifteen days after the election"—just before Thanksgiving Day—before counting soldier ballots. Of the nearly two million eligibles (troops over twenty-one) only 231,352 were able to cast their votes in the field, overwhelmingly for Lincoln. The others missed out by choice, lack of opportunity, bureaucratic failures, or design. Yet via their contacts with home, they influenced the entire national vote, counted as 4,034,789. Lincoln's popular majority was a relatively close half a million. His lopsided electoral total—the way the system often works—was 212 to McClellan's 21.

Neither candidate, servicemen knew, would get them home by Christmas, but Lincoln had matured in soldiers' minds from dismaying amateur in the White House to Father Abraham. When the reelection news belatedly reached Belgium, and the Union frigate *Niagara* in Antwerp harbor—the Atlantic cable, frayed and broken before the war, was still unrepaired—Commander Thomas T. Craven wrote to Secretary of the Navy Gideon Welles, "The *Niagara* was immediately dressed with our national flag, flying at her masthead. . . . At noon [I] fired a salute of twenty-one guns. It is, I believe, the first time since our national existence, that such a demonstration was made by any of our ships of war; but the occasion seemed so momentous and all glorious to me, that I could not resist the impulse to thus manifest my joy."

The national flag now carried thirty-five stars, one more than at the beginning of the war in 1861. In Virginia, the western counties had broken away to form a new state. The eleven Rebel secessions went unrecognized, while Nevada, marginal in population and hastily admitted to the Union on October 31, 1864, had not been added to the thirteen stripes. It seemed likely that the Union flag would keep all its stars, old and new.

TWO

Marching from Atlanta

LOOKING BACK, BUT NOT LIKE LOT'S WIFE WITH any desire to return," Union Sergeant Rice C. Bull of the 123rd New York, a young upstate farmer twice wounded at Chancellorsville, wrote with biblical imagery on November 15, "we could see the smoke and flames of the burning city rise to the sky. It was yet early morning, there was little wind and the smoke hung like a great pall over the doomed town we had just left. . . . Soon we were out of sight of burning Atlanta but the smoke rose in black columns and was visible all day."

The brigade band of the 33rd Massachusetts played the "Miserere" from Giuseppe Verdi's *Il Trovatore* that evening. Major Hitchcock confided to his diary that the music would thereafter always carry him back to exiting Atlanta. First performed in America only nine years earlier, the opera had reached a broad urban public. Its "Miserere" choral lament—the prayer from a prison tower of the condemned Manrico that peace attend his soul—was already familiar. Although the unfortunate troubadour sings, "Light me to early death," the implications of "Miserere" in the context of devastated Georgia were almost certainly lost on the bluecoat bandsmen, as was the irony of their playing "Home, Sweet Home."

In Richmond, Jefferson Davis claimed that the South was "as erect and defiant as ever"—that the Confederacy would regain Atlanta. It would, and soon, for occupying the battered city was out of the question for Sherman. Atlanta was now a geographical burden rather than a glittering prize. Maintaining troops there to be supplied over 120 miles of risky rail lines from Chattanooga made little sense. More useful was Sherman's detaching a force for oversight of Hood's grays from Tennessee, and foraging off the land in fertile Georgia at harvest time while pushing eastward to the sea. Hood's gambit in moving north was intended to draw troops after him and away from Georgia, but Sherman had sent only the men and matériel he would not need further to Major General George H. Thomas in Nashville. One Tennessee family had already postponed its last Christmas until January, ". . . the yankees seeing fit to spend Christmas with us." They would have to do so again.

Sherman's last message had been from Thomas—a telegram dated November 12 about Confederate troop dispositions. "You will have," Thomas advised confidently, "at least a clear road before you for several days. . . . Your success will fully equal your expectations." Sherman wired back, "Dispatch received—all right." To Grant he had already telegraphed that he would "trust to the Richmond papers to keep you well advised." Then, at Sherman's instructions, his Federals "burnt a bridge, which severed the telegraph-wire [across], and all communications with the rear ceased thenceforth."

Savannah, but for the turns and twists en route, was about three hundred miles to the southeast. The two prongs of Sherman's forces, purged of the wounded, the sick, and others judged unfit for the campaign and entrained north, numbered 62,204 effectives, including 5,062 cavalry and 1,812 artillerymen. Each regiment at full strength comprised 1,025 men, including 39 officers. A brigade included four regiments, and a division consisted of three or four brigades. Both of Sherman's wings had two corps, each composed of two or more divisions. Hundreds of wagons drawn by mules followed with basic rations for twenty days. Also in the train were ten thousand cattle on the hoof for which forage would be needed after the first five days, to provide fresh meat in the field. To stretch supplies, every man and every animal would have to live off the land. "We won't starve in Georgia," Sherman assured his wife. "Our mules are doing better on the cornfields than on the bagged corn brought by the Railroads."

On November 12 he had advised Ellen, in a letter for the last railway train north, not to write again until she heard from him. Yet he had given his goal away more than once. "I propose to abandon Atlanta and the railroad back to Chattanooga," he had telegraphed on October 19 to Amos Beckwirth, his acting chief quartermaster, "to sally forth to ruin Georgia and bring up on the seashore." Both sides tapped the telegraph wires and intercepted mail. Yet to Fleet Captain Alexander Pennock of the Mississippi Squadron, who managed the flow of captured cotton upriver from New Orleans to Cairo, Illinois, the general wrote on November 3: "In a few days I will be off for salt water and hope to meet my old friend [Rear Admiral] D[avid] D. Porter again. Will you be kind enough to write him and tell him to look out for me about Christmas, from Hilton Head to Savannah."

Both to bluff the Confederates and to broaden opportunities for foraging, Sherman's right (or lower) wing under Major General Oliver Otis Howard was to march ostensibly toward Macon, while Major General Henry W. Slocum's left wing was to feint toward Augusta but actually target the Georgia capital, Milledgeville. The armies would move roughly in parallel, thirty to sixty miles apart. In that swath, Private

Upson would write, they would leave "mighty few fences," as the slats and posts were prime firewood.

Where Sherman was heading proved, beyond the message to Pennock, to be no secret. An army that large and strung out for miles could not be hidden. Since its pace was limited not only by soldiers' legs but by straining mules and lowing cattle, enemy cavalry scouts could warn the immediate targets. Until telegraph wires and railway tracks were severed, Confederate defenders remained well informed, although largely drained of replacements. A traveler to Augusta told the *Chronicle*, which considered it news, that when Sherman was evacuating most white residents to the south, a woman, to appear mulatto, boiled walnut shells and dyed her hands and face. Safe, then, to make inquiries, she found out from chatty Federals that they would be leaving soon, so they thought, toward Macon and Augusta.

Union officers were to blame for some blown secrecy. Even Sherman may have been too free in his banter with underlings. Just as the columns began moving eastward, the Northern press reported details that were much too accurate. On November 8, as troops were preparing to move eastward and nonessential goods and troops were being ordered north, the *Indianapolis Journal* published a dispatch under a Cincinnati dateline with an estimate of Sherman's march strength and intentions. Augmented further, the story was picked up the next day by the *New York Times* and other Union newspapers, and immediately after by the Richmond press. From Virginia, Grant telegraphed Secretary of War Stanton indignantly that the *Times* version was "the most contraband news I have seen published during the war."

Stanton guessed that Sherman himself, despite his penchant for secrecy and plans for a news blackout, was to blame. "There is reason to believe," Stanton told Grant, "that he has not been very guarded in his own talk. I saw to-day, in a paymaster's letter to another officer, [Sherman's] plans as stated by himself. Yesterday I was told full details given by a member of his staff to a friend in Washington. Matters not spoken of aloud in the [War] Department are bruited by officers coming [home to vote] from Sherman's army in every Western [newspaper] printing office. . . . If he cannot keep from telling his plans to paymasters, and his staff are permitted to send them broadcast over the land, the Department cannot prevent their publication."

Berating the hero of Atlanta when even the lauded Grant was mired short of Richmond was impossible. Rather, Stanton had Assistant Secretary Charles Dana telegraph to Sherman on November 9, when the embarrassing news broke: "Indianapolis Journal says: 'Officers from Chattanooga report that Sherman returned to Atlanta early last week with five

Howard.   Kilpatrick.   Logan.   Hazen.   Sherman.   Jeff C. Davis.   Slocum.   Blair.   Mower.

SHERMAN AND HIS GENERALS

corps of his army, leaving two corps in Tennessee to watch Hood. He destroyed the railroad from Chattanooga. . . . Atlanta was burned, and Sherman is now marching for Charleston, S.C.'"

Sherman wired back to Dana to demand that the "fool" who gave the story to the papers be sent to him to do hard labor "on the fort[ification]s." Then he telegraphed again, more seriously: "If indiscreet newspaper men publish information too near the truth, counteract its effect by publishing other paragraphs calculated to mislead the enemy, such as 'Sherman's army has been re-enforced, especially in the cavalry, and he will soon move several columns in circuit, so as to catch Hood's army [in Tennessee].'" He suggested, alternatively, "Sherman's destination is not Charleston, but Selma[, Alabama], where he will meet an army from the Gulf [at Mobile]."

Dana ordered a search for the culprit, but no informer was identified. Much of what the Northern press reported that was not from Confederate sources was dismissed in the South anyway as intended to mislead.

Commanding the right column of two corps, the taciturn Major General Howard was as unlike Sherman as it was possible to be. Captain Charles Wills of the 103rd Illinois, deficient in spelling as were many Federals, recalled the usually disheveled Sherman as he rode by—and he would switch from wing to wing during the march—as resembling "somb oald plow jogger[,] his head bent a little to one side[,] with an oald stub of a[n unlit] sigar in his mouth." Wrinkled from sun and wind, and with a short, scruffy reddish beard going gray, he looked older than his forty-four years. Beneath his brown linen shirt and unkempt uniform jacket and breeches, Sherman wore faded red flannel undershirts and drawers.

Oliver O. Howard, a bearded New Englander who became postwar director of the Freedmen's Bureau and helped to establish a black university in Washington, D.C., that would bear his name, was as fervent for abolition as Sherman was dubious about racial equality. A West Point graduate in 1854, and its superintendent in the early 1880s, Howard had lost his right arm with the Army of the Potomac. He had fought at Bull Run and Antietam, and was routed by Stonewall Jackson at Chancellorsville. Howard did not smoke, drink, or swear, and kept his tunic with its shortened empty sleeve tightly buttoned. After Major General James McPherson, a Sherman protegé, was killed near Atlanta, Grant assigned "Old Prayerbook" to Sherman to command the Army of the Tennessee, now Sherman's right wing.

Henry Slocum, a lean, broadly mustached, trim-bearded New Yorker who at forty-two was already graying, had returned to duty after leaving the prewar army to practice law. Wounded at Manassas (Bull Run), he stoutly covered the retreat from Second Manassas, and led divisions at Chancellorsville, Gettysburg, and Vicksburg. His thirty thousand troops in two corps, renamed the Army of Georgia as a parallel to Howard's army, had been the first to enter Atlanta. On the morning of November 16, mounted on fast-stepping Sam, his favorite horse, Sherman and his small staff, accompanied by a cavalry escort, would join the march toward the rear of Slocum's left column. As troops cantered east on smoky, burned-out Decatur Street, a band played "John Brown's Body." Other regimental bands took it up, and men in the ranks sang lustily.

Not long after, units of the left wing, leaving Covington, passed through Shady Dale, a crossroads village where wealthy planters had clustered their posh residences. To Brigadier General William P. Carlin, an Illinoisan in XIV Corps, the hamlet radiated "comfort, wealth, and elegance," but the landowners had fled. "I saw no white people. . . . The column was halted a short time in the village and the band of one of the regiments struck up 'John Brown's body lies moldering in his grave, but his soul goes marching on.' To us there was nothing new in this, but what was new and striking was that a large number of young Negro girls—probably a dozen—came out from the several mansions in the vicinity, formed into a ring around the band at the head of the column, and with a weird, plaintive wail danced in a circle in a most solemn, dignified and impressive manner. There was not a man in this dance, nor was there a word spoken . . . between any of these girls and the officers or men of my command." Although puzzled, Carlin "interpreted it as expressive of good will. . . . The modest and serious deportment of those girls . . . produced a favorable impression on me, and doubtless on others who witnessed it."

The general did not realize that the curious performance was being repeated for each unit marching through Shady Dale. Puzzled, Michael Dresbach, a Minnesota soldier, would write to his wife that "15 young Wenches came out and danced for every Regiment . . . , the Brigade Band playing w[h]ile Each Brigade passed and the next one in turn taking its place. The way they hoed down [was] a caution and extremely ludicrous." However odd it seemed to him, the slave girls were expressing, in their plantation dance, authentic joy. In most plantations, slaves were permitted dancing only at Christmas, often swaying to the "camel walk" or the "buzzard lope." Remembered African excess did not promote meekness and obedience.

Slaves' Christmas practices were often incomprehensible even to their owners, as some blacks still sang, as they danced, songs of rejoicing in "Geechee," a pidgin of West African languages and English, and adapted in prayer traditional Protestant hymns into African rhythms. They fashioned their own stringed instruments, African style, from animal bladders and horsehair, and drummed on hide stretched tautly over hollow logs. Many believed, although they saw farm animals bellow and bleat daily, that on Christmas Eve the animals somehow kneeled, bellowed, and bleated in adoration and praise of Jesus. In Savannah on Christmas Eve, in better times, both blacks and whites danced to their separate tunes, often in carnivalesque garb, set off firecrackers in the streets, and threw blazing wads of kerosene-soaked cotton at each other. Such fireworks were now banned in Savannah and elsewhere. War had brought chaos enough.

* * *

THE CAVALRY, commanded by Hugh Judson Kilpatrick, who compensated for his lack of height by his swagger, was ostensibly under Sherman himself but difficult, when at a distance, to control. One of the youngest Union generals, "Lil' Kil" was disliked by his troops for putting them at excessive risk. After his West Point class of 1861 graduated early following the firing on Fort Sumter, he led cavalry in Virginia, proved useful at Gettysburg, and in mid-1864 was wounded in Georgia. Returning to action, he led a botched attack on railways south of Atlanta. Sherman admired his drive, although not his skirt chasing, conceding that Kilpatrick's self-promoted exploits left him "more than ever convinced that cavalry could not or would not work hard enough to disable a railroad properly, and therefore I resolved at once to proceed to the execution of my original plan."

Although since identified with Sherman, destroying rail lines was hardly original with him. As early as the first months of the war, Confederate orders in Virginia were to burn all railway bridges and connecting trackage behind them to prevent their use by the Federals. In Georgia, Sherman counted upon the efficiency of his engineering chief, Captain Orlando Poe, a West Pointer who graduated sixth in his class in 1856. Although he was a brigadier general of volunteers under McClellan after Second Bull Run, Congress—now hostile to McClellan—refused to confirm the promotion, and the mustached, goateed Poe had to revert to his regular army rank of captain. Only at the end of the war did he again wear a star, but the lack of it did not diminish his authority under Sherman. Poe's wreckage system—"Sherman's bow ties"—required a regiment of about a thousand men to line up along one side of a track and, on order, flip the wooden ties to jar the rails loose. The iron—of poorer quality than hardened Northern trackage—would be piled on a bed of felled telegraph poles and ties of Southern pine that burned like

SOLDIERS RIP UP A RAILROAD, BURN THE TIES,
AND WRAP THE HEATED RAILS AROUND A TREE

pitch. When the middle of a softened rail reddened, soldiers would pick up both ends and twist the track around a tree. For added pressure they employed a cant hook, Poe's ingenious wrenchlike device that warped the rails uselessly in opposite directions.

Poe's men sometimes bent heated rails into giant "U.S." letters and left them as a symbol of the essential powerlessness of the Confederacy. Since the destruction was to prevent a hostile force from being supplied, or moving toward the Federal rear as the army advanced, the operation was preventative as well as vindictive. No usable trackage, bridges, or unblocked roads were to be left to the rear of the bluecoat columns. Sherman had explained to Grant in making a case for his march, "It will be a physical impossibility to protect the roads, now that Hood, Forrest,

Wheeler and the whole batch of devils, are turned loose without home or habitation. . . . I propose that we break up the railroad from Chattanooga forward, and that we strike out with our wagons for Milledgeville, Millen, and Savannah. Until we can repopulate Georgia, it is useless for us to occupy it, but the utter destruction of its roads, houses, and people, will cripple their military resources. By attempting to hold the roads, we will lose a thousand men each month, and will gain no result. I can make this march, and make Georgia howl!"

"Fighting Joe" Wheeler's "critterbacks" were Sherman's chief impediment. The Federals did not anticipate direct confrontation, but their supply trains were ponderous, lengthy, and slow, and their flanks open to surprise attack wherever covering troops were insufficient. The fearless, flamboyant, five-foot-five Wheeler, three times wounded, was expert in harassing larger forces and sowing confusion. He vowed "death to all foragers," who risked, if captured, summary shooting. Rather than deter massive foraging, enemy harrying weeded out the least determined men. Sherman had two artists from *Harper's Weekly* accompany the troops, creating vivid images of the destruction of trackage, but they pictured only the return of foragers with their plunder. It was too risky to follow them into the unknown countryside.

For each day's march, Orlando Poe carried an odometer measuring the mileage. He had to estimate when pontoon-laden wagons would be needed forward to replace bridges destroyed by Confederate militia or local loyalists. Collapsible pontoons—wooden frames covered with canvas—could be transported efficiently in the supply train, then reused at the next fording of streams or swamps. Water was always Poe's engineering focus. He had been a prewar surveyor of the Great Lakes. Ironically, he would oversee the security of postwar transcontinental railway construction, warding off Indian tribes that wanted to do the damage Poe had done wholesale in the South.

Lumbering well behind Sherman were the artillery caissons, with

2,000 men and 65 cannon; 2,500 supply wagons, each drawn by 6 mules, and carrying over a million rations of hardtack biscuits, supplies of pork, coffee, salt and sugar; and 200 rounds of ammunition for each soldier to supplement the 40 each carried. (Coffee was especially prized, brewed by dropping beans into water brought to a boil. The beans were reused until drained of all flavor.) Officers were to carry no unnecessary personal gear, and Sherman's staff of five was not excepted. His own baggage was lean. His maps and papers and an inevitable book were in his pockets and saddlebags, along with a change of underwear, a flask of whiskey, and cigars. His dress uniform was somewhere back in the supply train.

All commanders down to company level were furnished with copies of field orders 119 and 120, dated November 8 and November 9, which were to be read to troops before the march. Although Sherman would write in his memoirs that the language was "clear and emphatic," he recognized its essential ineffectiveness. The orders, he recalled, "were obeyed as well as any similar orders were, by an army operating wholly in an enemy's country, and dispersed, as we necessarily were. . . ." His subordinates would have to enforce their authority over their strung-out forces as they could, or would.

Sherman's second order dealt mainly with the mechanics of the operation, restrictions (largely useless) on foraging, and warnings (often ignored) against entering residences, using "abusive or threatening language" to inhabitants, and looting personal property. The first order mandated the march, but left the targets unidentified. "It is sufficient for you to know," Sherman cautioned his troops, "that it involves a departure from our present base, and a long and difficult march to a new one. All the chances of war have been considered and provided for, as far as human sagacity can." He called for the maintenance of "that discipline, patience, and courage, which have characterized you in the past," with their goal of "the complete overthrow" of the enemy. He emphasized the hazards of straggling, of slipping away from the column for personal plunder. Soldiers might be caught by the enemy, or killed. Worse, from Sherman's standpoint, they might return to encumber wagons with "any thing but provisions and ammunition"—code for the booty soldiers loved to appropriate, largely material goods of momentary appeal, whatever their later fate. Few prizes would make it to Christmas.

To Southerners, Sherman was an anomaly as well as a mystery. As a militia colonel and prewar superintendent of the newly opened— with fifty-one cadets—Louisiana State Seminary of Learning and Military Academy (later relocated, and now LSU) he seemed to be a close cultural fit. An Ohioan and no slave owner, he was nevertheless outspoken that blacks were an inferior race, unready and unfit for citizenship. Belying the burgeoning secession climate, the motto of the school, inscribed above its main entrance, remained "The Union—*esto perpetua.*" But five days before Christmas in 1860, South Carolina had seceded, and on January 10, 1861, Louisiana militia seized the Federal arsenal at Baton Rouge. Sherman was ordered to accept a shipment of its guns, altered yet obsolete flintlock muskets. Although their value was little more than symbolic, he refused what he considered stolen goods, and eight days later wrote to Governor Thomas O. Moore, "If Louisiana [should] withdraw from the Federal Union, I prefer to maintain my allegiance to the Constitution as long as a fragment of it survives, and my longer stay here would be wrong. . . ." Yet the cautious language of the Constitution itself—evading reference to the actual word—permitted slavery, for the slave population in states to be persuaded into the initial Union helped determine (in the "three-fifths compromise") representation in a Congress in which blacks had no vote. A later, compensatory, article—to have it both ways—forbade importation, after 1807, of "persons held to service or labor." Southern states hoped to circumvent the ban.

Had slavery been held illegal, as many Northern delegates urged in

1787, no union of the thirteen original colonies could have happened. If Thomas Jefferson, a Virginia slave owner, had, as president, prohibited slavery in the Louisiana Territory, a bargain purchase from Napoleon in 1803, the South might then have seceded. Most of the fifteen presidents prior to Lincoln were slave owners. Congress remained dominated by Southerners, who ensured that compromises on admission of new states stretched slavery westward.

Sherman's own army service included stints in slave-owning Florida, Alabama, Georgia, South Carolina, and Louisiana, as the South dominated the military structure and its officer corps, and its forts and garrisons housed most Federal arms and munitions. Militias in the South, in part out of fear of local slave rebellions, were far more professional than their equivalents above the Mason-Dixon Line. The secretary of war under the dithering James Buchanan had been Jefferson Davis, now president of the Confederacy. The South could take a hard line about "state's rights," largely a euphemism for perpetuating slavery, but it could also point to the Constitution that Sherman championed. Despite the academy's motto, the founding document contained no clause denying a state the right to leave the Union. As Lincoln explained crisply, no government "ever had provision in its organic law for its own termination."

Sherman's replacement as academy superintendent would write to him, "Governor Moore desires me to express his profound regrets that the State is about to lose one who we all fondly hoped had cast his destinies for weal or for woe among us. . . ." The woe was accelerating. Sherman would write later to the army chief of staff, Henry Halleck, when Southerners loudly condemned the destruction in the wake of the march through Georgia, "If the people raise a howl against my barbarity and cruelty I will answer that war is war, and not popularity-seeking. If they want peace they and their relatives must stop the war." Living off the land was not the same as the excess of "teaching the home folks a lesson"—a form of pedagogy Sherman was employing but had not invented. Leaving only a legacy of hatred, pillage as punishment had not worked in previous wars and would not work then, nor has it since.

SHERMAN'S ARMIES divided between them 25,000 horses. Six hundred ambulance wagons, numbers that proved unnecessary, were each drawn by two horses. This was traveling light, with only the essentials for the campaign, yet in effect, two substantial cities were in motion, in parallel, for the lengthy trek through hostile country. Wagons had priority on the roads, where roads existed, with troops marching on both sides of the "train," often with additional animals. Orders permitted one pack mule per company, but some bluecoats would confiscate mules from Rebel farms.

Six men constituted a mess and divided the duties of carrying hatchet, coffeepot, camp kettle, "spider" (a fry pan with legs, to stand above burning coals), tin cups, and mess utensils. Each also had an overcoat, rubber poncho, blanket (often all in a roll), and spare stockings and underclothes. Private Upson wrote that "Of course, we [also] have our haversacks and canteens and our guns and cartridges boxes with 40 rounds of ammunition. Some of the boys carry 20 more in their pockets." The Federals expected little more than a few cavalry scouts to "scatter . . . at some crossroads or at a stream." Presumably they would be little bother. "Such an Army as we have I doubt if ever was got together before; all are in the finest condition. We have weeded out all the sick, feeble ones and all the faint hearted ones and all the boys are ready for a meal or a fight and don't seem to care which it is."

Troops anticipated an early Christmas through "secesh" loot they could carry off. The *New York Evening Post* correspondent accompanying the march had already watched soldiers "revel" in seized Rebel and foreign currency, little of it useful except as souvenirs unless it came in

FORAGERS STARTING OUT

the form of gold pieces. "Rebel money," he would write, "is so plentiful in camp that the men light their pipes with $50 bills, and kindle their fires with $5,000 Georgia State bonds." Sherman's orders authorized foraging "liberally on the country" by designated parties, usually squads of about twenty-five sent out in different directions so that coverage of farmsteads would be broad, and they could defend themselves; but he knew that commanders could not control bands intent upon sheer robbery, other than by recognizing that troops could carry away little that they could keep on their persons during the march. Soldiers would often fail that reality test, discarding bulky thefts, from silver plate to pictures and even pianos. March routes could soon be traced by the rubbish.

Sherman's loosely policed instructions to troops permitted destruction of mills and gins and other buildings likely to support the enemy economy or Rebel resistance, but no dwellings except where there seemed a threat within. Horses, mules, and wagons could be seized "freely and without limit," from "the rich, who are usually hostile," rather than from "the poor and industrious, usually neutral or friendly." Foragers were to leave families "a reasonable portion for their maintenance." That would not often happen. Captain Wills was soon calling the march "the most gigantic pleasure expedition," and a forager raiding a farm would explain to a weeping woman as the last of her flock was seized, "Madam, we're going to suppress this rebellion if it takes every last chicken in the Confederacy."

Unauthorized "bummers" would share little, even with the units from which they had deserted, and would burn on whim. Through Major George Ward Nichols, an aide to Sherman, *bummer* entered the language. He was quoted in the *Pall Mall Gazette* in London the next year as describing a bummer rather politely as "a raider on his own account—a man who temporarily deserts his place in the ranks . . . and starts upon an independent foraging expedition." With many of German ancestry in the ranks, the term apparently arose from *Bummler*, an idler who goes on a spree. "See hyar, cap'n," Nichols quoted an unashamed bummer; "we ain't so bad after all. We keep ahead of the skirmish line allers. We let's

FORAGERS RETURNING TO CAMP

'em know when the enemy's a-comin'; and we ain't allers away from the regiment. We turn over all we don't want ourselves, and we can lick five times as many Rebs as we are, any day."

The waste would have been scandalous had many on the march felt any shame, but everything seemed enemy property, for any resident along the route was by easy definition a Rebel. Watches and jewelry were coveted, then often stolen, bartered, or gambled from one soldier to another. Food, including that on the hoof, was eaten or abandoned. As he confided to his diary, Major Henry Hitchcock felt embarrassed at the ransacking yet realized that the campaign could not pause to decree wholesale punishments impossible to carry out. A Georgian would concede to Hitchcock "that the Confederates were a great deal worse than our men, that they pillaged and plundered everybody, and that inhabitants dreaded their coming." Nevertheless, embittered and sullen Confederate women blamed only the bluecoats for the privation and the chaos.

Sherman's estimate of forty days in the field before Christmas included brief respites for reorganization, for foraging, for fording or bridging streams, and for fighting off likely attacks, largely, he expected, from local militia. Hood's troops, two hundred miles to the northwest, had cut off Union forces from further supply; but, anticipating that, Sherman had already severed such links himself. To the east, fear spread among Georgians not only that the land would be stripped but that the Federals were unstoppable. From the threatened state capital of Milledgeville, Governor Joseph Brown had assured General Pierre Beauregard confidently that thirty thousand additional Georgians could be recruited.

Unable to extract even ten thousand men from those previously exempted for occupational or family reasons, Brown soon telegraphed Jefferson Davis in Richmond, more in hysteria than hope, to "send us troops as re-enforcements. . . . We have not sufficient force." Davis wired Major General Howell Cobb, commander of the Georgia Militia, once state governor, and President Buchanan's secretary of the treasury, owner of several plantations and five hundred slaves, to enlist every able-bodied white Georgian, and to employ blacks to fell trees and obstruct roads. Cobb had little success. Although they could not arrive in time even if released to him, Brown again implored Davis to send home the Georgia regiments in Virginia entrenched at Petersburg to defend Richmond.

With real news nearly nonexistent, and fed upon Southern pride, a Georgian in Lee's Army of Northern Virginia would later write home, on November 29, two weeks into the march: "It is the expectation of most every body that Sherman will be captured." In Columbia, South Carolina, where Mary Chesnut had moved from Richmond to accompany her husband, James, a brigadier general deputed by President Davis to the conscripting of reluctant South Carolinians, she deplored how "disaffected" she had learned recruits were. Those from hill country towns and farms "wanted peace—said this was a rich man's war—they had no part or lot in it, would gladly desert in a body. . . . Our returned prisoners were broken-spirited and said they had enough of it." She felt numbed—until her friend Malley Howell came in with a different spin on the way the war was going. "Our returned"—exchanged—"prisoners come back, fired with patriotism, and will fight this thing through to the death," he contended. "He was in such excellent spirits—mine rose, too. Then he showed us maps and traced with his finger how and where Sherman was sure to be bagged." She found herself believing him, although when she had last sat down to a wartime Christmas dinner at home in Virginia, served on "everything . . . that a hundred years or more of unlimited wealth could accumulate as to silver, china, glass, damask—&c&c" Mary Chesnut was already aware that her life as a plantation mistress was ending.

Closer to the action, the *Augusta Constitutionalist* saw the Federals as in retreat to some sanctuary on the seacoast, likening their situation to that described by Xenophon in his *Anabasis*, when ten thousand Greek mercenaries made a grim trek homeward from Persia in the early fourth century BC. Connecticut-born Nathan Morse of the *Augusta Chronicle* editorialized as early as November 13, before Sherman left Atlanta, that the general's safety lay in withdrawal. Other Southern newspapers had quoted Davis's boast, made on a fleeting visit to Macon, "Our cause is not lost. Sherman cannot keep up his long line of communication; and retreat sooner or later he must. And when that day comes, the fate that befell the army of the French Empire in its retreat from Moscow will be re-enacted. Our cavalry and our people will harass and destroy his army, as did the Cossacks that of Napoleon, and the Yankee general, like him, will escape with only a bodyguard." Trapping the Federals and then pushing their remnants "back to the banks of the Ohio," the Confederate president predicted, would "give the peace party in the North an accretion no puny [newspaper] editorial can give."

Very likely neither Davis nor anyone else, North or South, knew of the closest parallel to Sherman's march, as it occurred in China in 208 BC when the general Xiang Yu led his troops across the Yangtze River into enemy territory. When they debarked, he ordered his Zhao forces to pack three days' rations, then to crush their cooking pots and burn their boats. They were to push *forward*, living off the land. Retreat as in the *Anabasis* was not an option. In the summer of the next year, remnants of the defeated Qin army surrendered to Xiang.

AUTUMN RAINS were already pelting Georgia as Sherman prepared to march. On Election Day in the North, but carefully leaving that event unmentioned, he had sent messages to his commanders down the line, referring only to the weather, "This is the rain I have been waiting for and as soon as it is over we will be off." Learning of Davis's remarks about Napoleon's winter nightmare far from home, Grant scoffed, "Who is to furnish the snow for this Moscow retreat?" A retreat suggests a pursuer. Hood's moves into the vacuum Sherman left behind were unlikely, as he had to contend with George Thomas in Tennessee at his own rear. Having deliberately closed off his own return routes, Sherman could only press forward, toward the sea, with his caravan of supply wagons and rations on the hoof possibly vulnerable to surprise skirmishes and harassing Rebel horsemen. Miles ahead, the rain would mire even further the swamps and marshes that surrounded much of Savannah.

SHERMAN HAD WRITTEN his orders limiting destruction ambiguously, to permit seizing or burning of anything likely to be useful to the enemy. His language left room for ravaging nearly everything, and there were Confederate precedents. The year before, the Johnny Rebs had left a path of plunder and arson through Maryland and southern Pennsylvania en route to Gettysburg, even forcing free blacks south into slavery. Hood had put his own torch to Atlanta before the Federals came the next summer, and Jubal Early's 15,000 grays had vandalized the Shenandoah Valley during the summer before withdrawing southward—robbing banks and demanding ransom. (Union greenbacks were valuable and Confederate paper nearly worthless.) Two of Early's cavalry brigades burned Chambersburg, Pennsylvania, when its residents did not come up with $500,000 demanded as restitution for alleged Union depredations in Virginia. The pre-Atlanta forays in the North had enabled the stubbornly Confederate-leaning *Times* of London to claim that the South was "more formidable than ever."

Since his leaving Atlanta, the Northern press had no news of Sherman but for rumor, speculation, and dispatches from unreliable Confederate sources. Major Hitchcock had incautiously made a seacoast destination obvious in a letter to his wife when he wrote just before the march, "You may not hear of us save through the rebel papers for a time—perhaps my next letter will come by New York." At her plantation in North Carolina south of Roanoke, Catherine Ann Edmondston, anxious for news, wrote in her diary, "Not one word from Hood & the Yankees are equally ignorant about Sherman. For the first time since the invention of the Telegraph, says the *[Richmond] Examiner,* 'two large armies have disappeared whol[l]y from sight.'"

Much later, soldiers learned that the Union states had been following the scattered and unreliable reports of their progress with puzzled fascination. "We got some Northern papers today," Private Upson would write in his diary at Christmas. "It seems that the good people up there were terribly worried about us. They called us the *Lost Army.* And some thought we would never show up again. I don't think they know what kind of an Army this is that Uncle Billy has. Why, if Grant can keep Lee and his troops busy we can tramp all over the Confederacy; and by the time we were through with that, there would be nothing left but the ground. And that would be in a state primeval."

THREE

The Long Picnic

L EAVING LITTLE BUT THE GROUND IN SOME SEC-
tors, Sherman was attempting to make his destination uncertain until it became inevitable. His troops
moved between, but only threatened, Augusta and Macon,
cutting telegraph lines rather than employing them first to
confirm progress. Understanding Uncle Billy's silences, Grant
quipped to newsmen, "Sherman's army is now somewhere in
the condition of a ground mole when he disappears under
a lawn. You can here and there trace his track, but you are
not certain where he will come out until you see his head."
Lincoln fended off inquiries from reporters with, "We all
know where he went in at, but I can't tell where he will come
out at."

Without massive troop increments from the Carolinas or
Alabama, Major General William J. Hardee realized, his un-
derstrength scratch command in Savannah would have its
fate determined by Christmas. A Georgian and a West Pointer

who had fought in the Mexican war and published a book on infantry tactics, he was also a veteran of Shiloh, Chickamauga, and Chattanooga. When, after Atlanta, Hood marched north to Tennessee, Hardee was transferred to defend Savannah. Reinforcements, if any, would be meager, as middle and eastern Georgia was a land of women, children, old men, and slaves of every age and description who harvested the flourishing fall crops. Some of the younger whites who had evaded conscription were now inducted into Home Guard units in Augusta, Macon, or Savannah. Others—those with money or family connections—fled toward the apparent safety of South Carolina or Florida. Few stayed.

"Weather fine for marching," Major Hitchcock noted as he cantered out of Atlanta with the left wing, following the trackage, afterward torn up, toward Decatur and Covington. It was 7:00 AM, and overcast, on the sixteenth. "One fellow very drunk, sitting on ground as we passed troops. . . . Cursed General loudly. . . . General [Sherman] rode quietly by him, not ten f[ee]t off—heard all—no notice."

Decatur had been hammered earlier that summer during the siege of Atlanta. Textile mills and cotton gins spared earlier, or repaired, were now torched. Anxious Georgians to the east would assess the daily progress of the Federals by the approaching columns of smoke. (The gaunt chimneys left standing amid the smoldering ruins became known ruefully as "Sherman's sentinels.") Following a pause at Decatur, Slocum's left wing continued on until four in the afternoon, when troops began pitching tents in orchards and fields within sight of the round granite monolith of Stone Mountain. Then—as darkness came early in late autumn—they foraged wholesale for dinner. While frightened families in the path of the columns huddled indoors, soldiers bayoneted or clubbed "secesh" pigs, sheep, and chickens to roast with sweet potatoes and corn from the fields.

Howard's parallel right wing pushed toward the town of McDonough, while Kilpatrick's brigade (often called a division but less than divisional size) fended off Rebel horsemen attempting to burn bridges that Federals might cross. The left wing had made seventeen miles. Cotton bales were slashed open and laid out for bedding—a practice continued nightly while bluecoats were in cotton country. Elsewhere, troops made mats of straw or pine needles topped by blankets. After cutting tent poles from small trees or from branches they stripped, three soldiers would share a canvas fly tent, ditched around to carry rainwater off, and its sides buttoned together with an end flap. Campfires near the open end of the tent were fed with dry fence slats and barn siding. Warily, soldiers slept in their clothes, posted pickets, and awoke gratefully to the glow of fading embers and the noises of reassembly for the day's march.

At dawn on the seventeenth, the abandoned bedding was set afire, and on the left the march resumed toward Lithonia, with rails along the route heated with lifted ties and twisted into "Sherman's neckties." Just beyond, Hitchcock and staff stopped to rest at the farmhouse of Mrs. Scott, a war widow, "say thirty-five, civil and disposed to talk. She told [Captain Joseph] Audenreid that at Atlanta we had shot, burned, and drowned negroes, old and young, drove men into houses and burned them, etc.: first said she believed it, then admitted she did not, but wanted the negroes to believe it. . . . She says the niggers are the only free ones now—whites all slaves, 'in our country and yours too.'" Ahead of them troops foraged liberally. "Laughable to see pigs in feed troughs [wheeled] behind wagons, chickens swinging from knapsacks."

On the right, the armies halted at the Ocmulgee River until wagons loaded with planking arrived to repair damaged bridges. It would take all day, and into the night, for troops and herds to cross. A Rebel dispatch to Savannah from Macon reported the crossing as seeming "to strengthen the belief that Augusta is their object."

Chilly downpours, beginning on November 19, were bogging down both columns in thick mud. At nightfall there were few dry twigs to start fires. The 10th Michigan, detailed to drive cattle in the rear, was the last to set up camp, and Corydon ("Cord") Foote, a drummer boy who had enlisted the day after his thirteenth birthday in 1862, recalled a red-bearded veteran in cape and slouch hat standing over Company F, watching. As Cord dropped to his knees to blow the sputtering twigs into flame, the scruffy old soldier advised, "Try a poncho over it, boys, and I think you'll get it." He reached out to help hold it, and the flames flickered. "There, you have it," he said, pleased.

Recognizing him, Foote blurted boldly, despite his surprise, "Thank you, Uncle Billy." Shakespeare (in *Henry V*) had written of "a little touch of Harry in the night." That Sherman would turn up in such bardic fashion, his staff discreetly in the shadows, made his men willing to do anything for him, and he knew it. He also knew not to push his troops too far or too fast. He estimated that ten to fifteen miles per day to move, camp, feed, and regroup sixty thousand men and thousands of slower animals, was excellent progress toward Savannah by Christmas.

On the twentieth, Howard's bluecoats moved through Clinton to Gordon, feinting southward toward Macon to draw off defenders, if any, while Slocum's wing surged to Covington. There an officer looked in at the Travis household and asked Allie Travis and her sister, "Knitting socks for the Rebs?" Their balls of wool were wrapped round gold watches, concealing them from Union souvenir hunters. Another soldier joined to harangue them uselessly about the sin of secession; then a family friend arrived to suggest that they go to the porch to hear a passing brigade band playing "Dixie."

"They must be at a loss for tunes," Allie sneered; "they're playing one of ours." Almost as if they heard her, the bandsmen switched to "Yankee Doodle." The Travis ladies, unaware that "I Wish I Was in Dixie" was a blackface minstrel song originating in Ohio in the 1850s, scurried back inside, shut the door violently, and pulled down the blinds.

Sherman knew that he was already an object for special hatred in Georgia. "I doubt if history affords a parallel to the deep and bitter en-

A MORTAR BATTERY ON THE EDGE
OF A FEDERAL ENCAMPMENT

mity of the women of the South," he wrote to his wife, Ellen. "No one who sees them and hears them but must feel the intensity of their hate. Not a man is seen; nothing but women with houses plundered, . . . desolation sown broadcast, servants all gone and women and children bred in luxury, beautiful and accomplished, begging with one breath for the [pillaged] soldiers' rations and in another praying that the Almighty or Joe Johnston will come and kill us, the despoilers of their homes and all that is sacred."

Even the exploited slaves upon whose backs that comfortable way of life was built were not exempt from the plundering. While the Federals were passing, a black girl on the Travis homestead screamed that one of the men was clutching an armful of clothes she recognized as stolen from her cabin. A "Dutchman" still in the house—to Southerners, Union troops of German extraction, *Deutsch* in the North, were "Dutch"—

asked what was the matter "wid dat nigger," and Allie said scornfully, "Your soldiers are carrying off everything she owns, and yet you pretend to be fighting for the Negro." When another bluecoat came by jauntily wearing the slave girl's Sunday hat, she rushed up and shook her fists in his face, shouting, "Oh! If I had the power like I've got the will, I'd tear you to pieces!"

Such loot was easily seized and easily discarded, but Dolly Hunt Burge's thousand pounds of meats ransacked from her smokehouse, and her butter, eggs, pickles in brine, jugs of wine and syrup, squealing young pigs, and flapping chickens would be loaded into supply wagons to supplement rations. As the Federals had approached her plantation, she prayed that God "remember thy promise to the Widow & Orphan," but "like Demons they rush in." Appealing to a soldier she was told, "I cannot help you, Madam; it is the orders." Also seized were "Old Dutch," her buggy horse; "Old Mary," her brood mare; two colts and a mule; and even her daughter Sadai's doll, Nancy. Slave cabins were rifled of coffeepots, skillets, and Sunday clothes. "A Col. From Vermont" stationed two men to protect the little she had left, but they spoke German and she could not understand "one word they said." The pair lay by her fireplace through the night. When they awakened and rejoined their column, Dolly, stocky, middle aged, and nearly alone but for her slaves, surveyed what remained. All the meat she had left was on the discarded backbone of a hog.

Just after dawn, with all her fences and garden palings stripped for campfires, she sullenly watched the troops leave, a march that would take most of the day. For Mrs. Burge's breakfast, her women cooked a chicken found shot and abandoned.

On the Tuesday following—the Federals had left on a Saturday—Dolly walked wearily to "my graveyard . . . to see if it had been molested." She "rejoiced" that her husband had been spared "the destruction of his lifelong labor." A dead hog lay nearby. After a wearying circuit of four miles Mrs. Burge found some of her sheep alive in a swamp.

Sherman took the depredations lightly as the economic consequences of rebellion. Near one prosperous plantation a soldier passed him with a ham impaled on his bayonet, a jug of molasses under one arm while his other hand held a chunk of honeycomb. With no way to salute, he merely turned Sherman's order, "Forage liberally on the country," back at him. Sherman said nothing, but Major Hitchcock, riding alongside, read his impassive expression: "General sober as a judge." Among the lighter tales told of Sherman during the march, almost certainly untrue, was that of foragers running off with an old woman's poultry. Seeing Sherman riding by, the lady ran to the road and cried out, "General, your men are taking all my chickens!"

"Oh, yes," he conceded. "They will have to roost very high."

The depredations were far from funny. Sherman's orders protecting private residences "from any trespass" were often ignored. Unamused, Captain George W. Pepper, an Ohioan, described a typical episode as "A halt at noon beside a village, a besieging of houses by the troops, soldiers emerging from doorways and backyards, bearing quilts, plates, poultry and pigs, beehives attacked, honey in the hands and besmearing the faces of the boys, hundreds of soldiers, poking hundreds of bayonets in the corners of yards and gardens, after concealed treasure; here and there a shining prize, and shouting and scrambling, and a merry division of the spoils. In the background, women with praying hands and beseeching lips unheeded."

IN PROSPEROUS MADISON, a town of three thousand where the left wing briefly feinted toward Augusta and the northeast, a committee of elders led by former congressman Joshua Hill surrendered the town, begging Henry Slocum to have his XX Corps spare family homes. Hill, who opposed secession, had resigned his seat when his state left the Union. Other Georgian officeholders in Washington merely left. His son had been killed in action that May, fighting for the Confederates, but the past now served Hill, who would be elected to the Senate after the war. Although the town largely escaped theft and the torch, four thousand Federals camped on the grounds of Emma High's plantation. In her home, a black cook was making gingerbread cakes for the children. Some soldiers nearby, under the spell of the aroma, came into the kitchen, lifted the hot gingerbread, and dropped compensatory coins in a tin pan as they left. The last of the men took the remaining cakes—and all the coins. The cook was in tears.

Departing troops burned the railway depot, jail, and warehouses. And Madison, widely known for its lush flower gardens, was picked clean of roses as the men marched off with blossoms decorating their hats and rifles. Frederick Price of Colonel Henry Barnum's command would write to his wife, "It was here that hundreds of slaves joined the Army, some with half a dozen children along with them." Sherman bridled at the unruly increment of "contrabands" from the big, absentee-owner plantations; but unable to be everywhere at once, he was powerless to fend off the joyful, self-liberated blacks. A hindrance in every way, they slowed the columns, fed off their provisions, and gridlocked wagons, caissons, carts, cattle, horses, and mules. Some able-bodied males were potentially useful for performing "pioneer" tasks of road and bridge repair, but officers failed to restrain the eager hordes all along the march routes who cried out, "Jubilee! Jubilee!" Sherman would be criticized in the North for his apparent inhumanity in forestalling the swarming blacks, where he could hold them back, from abandoning workplaces where they could continue to be fed and housed.

The Bible-taught multitudes had learned from Leviticus that in the Jubilee year (often to them, "Jubilo"), after forty-nine of labor, fields were to lie fallow and workers in bondage released. On the Liberty Bell itself, cast in 1751 to recall William Penn's Charter of Privileges, and rung in July 1776 to mark the Declaration of Independence, was inscribed the biblical mandate for Jubilee,* "Proclaim Liberty throughout all the land unto all the inhabitants thereof."

MANY OF THE SELF-LIBERATED SLAVES who flocked after the army as plantation discipline deteriorated carried "bundles and bags of clothing, bedding and cooking utensils on their heads," Illinois soldier Enoch Weiss noted in amazement. Some took with them an "assortment of animals and vehicles, limping horses, gaunt mules, oxen and cows, hitched to old wobbly buggies, coaches, carriages and carts." It did not occur to them that there were days ahead of creeks, rivers, and swamps to cross, for liberation was now. "The Darkies come to us from every direction," Private Upson wrote. "They are all looking for freedom but real[l]y dont seem to know just what freedom means. They all have a great desire to see General, or Massa Sherman. . . . They marched along by the side of the road singing their songs till some one told them the truth. However, despite all the discouragements we have a large following though General Sherman has tried in every way to explain to them that we do not want them, that they had better stay on the plantations till the war is ended." Major General John W. Fuller of XVII Corps recognized an elderly black who had cried out earlier as the columns of marchers passed, "Dar's millions of 'em—millions!" Although barefoot, he had caught up with them. "How far are you going, uncle?" Fuller asked.

"Why," said the old man. "I've jined!"

"Bring[ing] the Jubilee"—which rhymes with "Atlanta to the sea"—would make its way into "Marching Through Georgia," the most popular song of 1865. Its second chorus echoed what seemed the actuality as the armies proceeded:

---

*   The word is from the Hebrew for the ram's horn sounded to signal the year of liberty.

How the darkies shouted when they heard the joyful sound,
How the turkeys gobbled which our commissary found,
How the sweet potatoes even started from the ground,
While we were marching through Georgia.

The Bible's language was appropriated by Southern whites as well as blacks. As General Howard's infantry on the right wing, with General Kilpatrick's cavalry, reached Hillsborough on the nineteenth, a squad of Rebel horsemen, seeking breakfast at the Cornwell plantation, saw smoke foreshadowing the Federals. The Rebels remounted and dashed off as shots were exchanged. According to Louise Reese Cornwell, after the sounds of firing were lost in the distance, "the Yankees returned, leading two riderless horses." (Local accounts of Union losses, and depredations, however real, were always in excess of reality.) Through the day the troops passed, "Terrible as an army with banners." The line was from the Song of Solomon.

"They drove off every cow, sheep, hog, yea, indeed, every living thing on the farm—took every bushel of corn and fodder, oats and wheat—every bee gum, burnt the gin house, screw, blacksmith shop, cotton. . . . My dear old mother, who was old, began to fail under such excitement." Still, "Gen. Howard and staff officers came at tea time. We managed to have something to eat for that meal, which was the last for several days, and while Gen. Howard sat at the table and asked God's blessing, the sky was red from flames of burning houses. After tea was over, we cordially invited Gen. Howard to pass the night under our roof, but he politely declined, saying it was best for him to stay with his men."

Before departing for the evening, Union officers "played on the piano many pretty pieces and sang several pretty songs." When the troops resumed the march the next day, Howard "kindly offered us a guard, . . . which of course was readily accepted." Yet, Louise Cornwell derided,

"Upon our being told to get out of our house [as] they were going to burn it, we always replied, 'If you burn our house, you can burn us in it. You have taken everything we possessed, now burn us up if you will, for we will not get out.' So it was left. . . ."

Since rumor had it that the Yankees burned all private houses in their path, Mrs. Elizabeth Pye, who lived near Hillsborough, in a panic had all of her furniture, including a large feather bed, concealed in the woods nearby. According to Captain Wills, foragers of the 103rd Illinois found the hiding place and carried her possessions back for her. More realistic, but hopelessly so, was Mrs. Godkins, a Hillsborough lady whose husband was a surgeon in Hood's army. "Better, a thousand times better," she told the reporter from the *Cincinnati Commercial*, "to go back into this Union this year *with a little honor*, than to do it next year *in disgrace!* Sherman will destroy everything before that time."

The quiet grace at tea with Mrs. Cornwell; the "cordial" overnight invitation to Howard; the "kindly" offer of a guard, while nearby residences reportedly burned wholesale; the Cornwell plantation itself confiscated of everything edible and on the hoof, and then ruined; the family left nearly without food for days; and the house threatened with burning, yet protected; the return of household goods—all these juxtapose contradictions not easily reconciled, yet integral to the surreality of the march to the sea.

For four days, the two corps of Howard's army, with supply trains following, passed through and campfires dotted the fields at dusk. Parallel routes within each wing were essential, whatever the terrain. When topography forced columns to converge, the tailbacks, clogged with contrabands, were enormous. Howard's troops and wagons and beef on the hoof, plus Kilpatrick's horsemen, Howard wrote, if "stretched out, would have been thirty-seven miles long." In proceeding at such risk, he had to order constant watches on all flanks for Rebel spoiling attacks, day and night. Road accidents, such as the pitching over of a loaded wagon in a

A BUMMER

rut or the toppling of exhausted cattle and mules, delaying movement for hours, were a further hazard.

As the weather turned cold, rain changed to sleet. Chilled Georgians isolated by the march had little wood for fireplaces, as slaves who remained often failed to service them and there were few other hardy men. Further, many oxen, horses, and mules were gone and wagons burned to their axles. Most dreaded everywhere were the "stragglers," unruly self-appointed bummers who drifted to the rear to steal, intimidate, and destroy, and usually escaped punishment except when killed in the act. Bummers became adept at finding silver and jewelry buried for safekeeping outdoors, secreted in ponds and under pigpens, in newly dug graves and under fresh fence posts. No war was without stragglers bent upon profiting from chaos, and the larger the army the more they proliferated. When Major Hitchcock complained to Sherman about them, the general shrugged, "I have been three years fighting stragglers, and they are harder to conquer than the enemy."

"Only one thing that was at all pleasing," Mrs. Cornwell recalled, "and that was momentary only—Gen. [Francis] Blair's [XVII Corps] command when passing played 'Lorena' with variations." Like "Aura Lee," another sentimental ballad that only hinted at wartime, the lyrics recalled the many months of "life's pelting storms" and the "duty stern and piercing" that had parted the song's lovers. "Snow was on the grass again," but it mattered little, for "The past is in the eternal past," and what was to come was "dust to dust beneath the sod." For a moment, she wrote, "we enjoyed it, then looking around, seeing our desolation," the thought involuntarily surfaced, "This music plays her gayest airs as in mocking of our woe."

FROM SUNDAY INTO TUESDAY the twenty-second, Private Frederick Buerstatte of the 26th Wisconsin Regiment wrote in his diary, in German, the infantrymen slogged through Madison and beyond in rain, wind, and mud. To keep warm on the march, "we crowded ourselves quite close together." Snow fell west of Milledgeville, the state capital; puddles iced over. Roads became quagmires as the mud thawed. To the south, the right wing reached the tracks of the Macon & Savannah Railroad near Gordon, and the men of Major General Peter Osterhaus's XV Corps kept warm at bonfires of burning ties and heated trackage. The bushy-mustached Osterhaus, a German-born Missourian, had fled Prussia after the failed revolutions in 1848, turned to business, and risen in the state militia before war came. His accent remained strong. "Prave boys, I nefer saw such prave boys!" Osterhaus praised his troops.

Concerned further about the vulnerability of the strung-out wagon trains to attacks from Wheeler's horsemen, Howard ordered Osterhaus to divert a brigade from routine trackage mayhem to support Kilpatrick's cavalry guarding the Union flank near the whistle-stop station at Gris-woldville, a small factory town. With two cannon, 1,500 men of the 46th Ohio and the 97th Indiana under Brigadier General Charles C. Walcutt positioned themselves on a ridge at a farmstead, ripped up fence rails for a barricade facing open ground, and settled in to cook their after-noon meal. They were not "dreaming of a fight," Captain Wills recalled, "when lively musketry opened on the picket line, and in a minute our pickets came in flying." Soldiers scrambled from bubbling skillets to seize their new seven-shot Spencer repeating rifles* as Rebel artillery—twelve guns—hemmed them in. One loaded cannon was hit and blew up. Wal-cutt took a wound in the leg and was quickly replaced by R. F. Catterson, an Indiana colonel.

The Federals were confronting 4,400 men of the Georgia Militia un-der Major General P. J. Phillips, up from Macon, and drove off seven frenzied assaults from as close as forty-five yards. Never having encoun-tered repeating rifles before, Phillips assumed that he was facing an entire division. The Confederates broke in disorder, firing, as they fell back, well over the heads of the veteran Northerners, who quickly realized that they were facing green troops. At dusk the shattered attackers crept away, reaching Macon, twelve miles distant, after midnight. The Federals counted their casualties—14 dead and 62 wounded. Among the former, Private Upson recognized "Uncle Aaron" Wolford, patriarch of his regi-ment. Also left on the field were 51 Georgia dead and 472 wounded. It would be the only severe confrontation Union forces would face before their Savannah Christmas.

To Captain Wills the Rebel militia, despite their numbers, were "grey-haired and weakly looking men, and boys not over 15 years old." Upson

---

* Lincoln had tried out Christopher Spencer's "seven-shooter magazine rifle" on grounds near the Potomac on August 17. It was adopted; 200,000 were manu-factured by war's end.

found an injured boy of fourteen lying next to his father, two brothers, and an uncle, all dead. Corpses were buried in the field. The wounded who could be moved were taken to a brigade dressing station, and the others left for the likely return of Confederate aid teams from Macon. A hastily assembled, inexperienced lot, Willis wrote, "They knew nothing at all about fighting." Confederate Major F. W. Capers claimed to General Henry Wayne about the cadets plunged into the action, "There was fatigue and blood and death in their ranks but no white feather."

Wanting to do something special for Uncle Aaron, Upson remembered that he had seen a hollow log nearby. "We got it, split it in halves, put one in the grave in the sandy soil, put his lifeless body into it, covered it with the other half, filled up the grave and by the light of a fire we had built with the rails, marked on a piece of lumber his name, Company, and Regiment." Upson carefully pocketed Wolford's money, watch, and "well worn Testament" to send to his dead friend's wife and eight children. In Macon, brushing aside the skirmish as "contrary to my instructions" and "an unfortunate accident," Major General Gustavus Smith ordered the ineffective militiamen onto trains southward to Albany, then circuitously overland on foot via Thomasville to Savannah.

Hobbled by his wound, Walcutt proceeded toward Savannah in an ambulance wagon with other casualties.[†] "We marched over rough places and jolted along corduroy roads, yet all our wounded from this battle," Howard wrote, "were transported from Griswold Station to the sea without loss of life." Major Thomas Ward Osborn would write from Savannah, "We brought all our wounded with us in the ambulances . . . and what is surprising about this is we have never known men to do as well in hospital as they have in this train on the road." Fresh air and

---

†   Sherman's ambulances were covered two-horse spring wagons with benches on the sides for walking wounded, and room for three to lie on the padded floor, with three more suspended in hammock stretchers that hung above.

fellow feeling were better, it seemed, than insanitary conditions under a stifling roof.

However bumpy, roads improvised unevenly from felled trees were better than the heaving and freezing mud that congealed as it thawed. When Sherman had to resort to log-laid corduroy, he employed the most hardy former slaves who had clung to his columns. They supplemented his own pioneers. Sherman also improvised a human telegraph. As Howard recalled, "General Slocum communicated with me and with Kilpatrick by scouting parties moving across from Slocum's column to mine, the distance being in the neighborhood of ten or twelve miles."

The right wing continued on, tearing up the trackage of the Macon & Savannah Railroad as troops approached the Oconee River and pontooniers moved up to bridge it sturdily enough for cannon and cattle to

SHERMAN'S FIELD HEADQUARTERS AT DUSK

cross. On the eighth day of the march, the left wing was approaching Milledgeville. Riding with XIV Corps near Eatonton, Sherman and his staff stopped at the Farrar plantation, where the slaves—there were at least twenty—told them that their master had left for Milledgeville the week before "to help in the breastworks, and to fight." No fight would occur. Although the planter had vanished, officers asked Mrs. Farrar for lunch. She had little choice. Mrs. Farrar would be pretty, Hitchcock thought, had she not been so slatternly. Her husband was in the Rebel army, she said proudly, "from choice," Hitchcock wrote, "—the first woman who has not declared her husband was forced to go." Her blacks had told them that the master flogged his slaves with straps, the flat of handsaws, and paddles with holes, the better to sting, and put salt in their wounds. Yet they showed no signs of leaving. Since Mrs. Farrar was not the guilty party, Sherman assured her that her property would be left unharmed.

An unidentified lady at a plantation nearby had a somewhat different experience. A letter to her sister was published in the weekly *Countryman* in Turnwold, Georgia, described on its masthead as "Devoted to the Editor's Opinions." The "blue-coat scoundrels" did not "trouble" her much, except "coming near eating me out of house and home." Her pa's buggy was stolen, and all her turkeys and chickens, but for one hen. The five turkeys were "very fat—in good Christmas order." Only two slaves left them; yet all her uncle's "negroes" went off "but one," a ten-year-old girl. "I feel very sorry for her." As for her father's country store in Eatonton, "You never saw such a complete wreck. . . . There was not a five cents' worth left in it." (*Countryman* could also excoriate its own side, quoting a Screven County lady identified only as Bertha that while the enemy "were burning and destroying property on one side of Brier Creek," Wheeler's cavalry "were stealing horses and mules on the other side.")

Mrs. Farrar's slaves had reported a "track hound" at the next plantation, a large reddish animal that its master employed to hunt down run-aways. Major Nichols whispered something to Sherman, who nodded. Soon they heard the dog's dying howls, and the blacks were "in great glee." A day earlier, Chaplain Tom Stevenson of the 78th Ohio wrote, "we passed the plantation of a Mr. Stubbs. The house, cotton gin, press, corn-ricks, stables, everything that could burn was in flames, and in the dooryard lay the dead bodies of several bloodhounds that had been used to track and pull down negroes and our escaped prisoners. And wherever our army has passed, everything in the shape of a dog has been killed. The soldiers and officers are determined that no more flying fugitives, white men or negroes, shall be followed by track-hounds. . . ."

"THE REBS," the slaves had warned, will give battle to defend Milled-geville, and had been fortifying it "ever since two years ago." Although Sherman often asked for directions, and information, from blacks rather than whites, assuming that slaves were less likely to mislead, he was skeptical that the capital would be defended, as its government buildings were more likely to survive if not fought for. He sent Orlando Poe forward with a squad to burn the Eatonton cotton mill and any bales in storage. "Thirty or forty" women who worked the spindles begged to have it spared, as it was their livelihood, but once the march continued, Poe felt, the factory might again produce uniforms for the Johnnies. Despite heavy rain, the mill was torched.

Hitchcock was continually appalled by the apparent inhumanity in Sherman's grim logic. Depriving the innocent of earnings, and exacerbating their miseries to drive home the hopelessness of the Rebel cause, seemed misplaced vengeance upon the dependents of the actual Rebels. "It is a terrible thing," he conceded to his diary, "to consume and destroy the sustenance of thousands of people, and most sad and distressing to see and hear the terror and grief and want of these women and children. . . . But if that terror and grief and want shall help to paralyze their husbands and fathers who are fighting us . . . it is mercy in the end."

On the column's sixth day out, the roads were worse and the weather, to Hitchcock, "horrible." In such conditions, the march could not resume until about eleven. Still, Sherman remained confident that he could reach the coast by Christmas. More than seventy-five miles from Atlanta now, his armies were ahead of schedule. Since the ruts were "fully 18 to 24 inches deep through stiff heavy red clay, some half-liquefied, some like wax, or thickened molasses," Hitchcock wondered how "heavy teams" could get through without dry weather or massive corduroying.

By evening a raw wind had blown the storm away, and the first stars were out. Sherman camped for the night on the Vann plantation, west of Milledgeville. To the general, Vann claimed, perhaps to protect his property, that the country was quietly Unionist, as he was. He professed disappointment that the state legislature hadn't done "something for peace." Vann's plantation was well stocked, but an officer with Sherman remarked skeptically that it was "a matter of severe doubt whether there will be much left."

On the seventh day out Sherman was with Major General Jefferson C. Davis's XIV Corps when the column camped at four only ten miles from the state capital. Davis, a glum, bearded, politically influential Kentuckian often confused with the Confederate president, was a less familiar figure than his namesake, known largely because two years earlier he had shot and killed Major General William Nelson during an argument in a Louisville hotel lobby. Davis was never prosecuted. As far as Sherman was concerned, the impulsive Davis was an effective commander, even punishing bummers summarily when the looting was extreme and his temper boiled over. Two men caught pilfering dresses were remanded to his provost marshal and marched behind slow provisions wagons in their filched frocks, wearing placards on their backs announcing, "STOLEN." Others on the order of one of his captains had to carry heavy bags of sand for twenty days on the march and wear placards labeled "ROBBER."

On the raw, cold afternoon of November 22, eight days out, Sherman reached a sprawling plantation on the outskirts of Milledgeville. His staff built a fire where they expected to settle in as darkness loomed. Calling for his orderly and saddlebags, Sherman poured some warming whiskey for himself, lit a cigar, and walked toward a row of log slave cabins while waiting for the headquarters wagon with its dinner rations. When an elderly black woman saw the soldiers making camp, she advised Sherman that he would find "a better place" down the road. Farther on was a house in which he found some of his officers already at a blazing fireplace. As he sent word to bring horses and wagons up he noticed a small box, "like a candle-box," marked "Howell Cobb." Asking a slave, Sherman found that they were at "Hurricane," one of the several farmsteads of the commander of the Georgia Militia. With the property at hazard, Cobb had evacuated fit slaves from its six thousand acres, abandoning fifty women, children, and old men, and—as he was short of transport—a hoard of corn, oats, beans, peanuts, twenty sacks of prized salt and five hundred gallons of sorghum molasses. Cobb was the "head devil," Hitchcock advised. Sherman ordered produce that could be foraged loaded on the supply train.

After supper, he recalled in his memoirs, as he sat astride a chair at the fireplace, he saw an elderly slave peering at his face, and trembling. "Dis Mr. Sherman? Master, please give me dat light!" The general handed a candlestick to him for a closer look "Well—well—and dis is Mr. Sherman!" he convinced himself. "I shan't git done bein' skeered all day tomorrow!" He explained that he wanted to be certain that they were indeed Yankees. He had been dreaming about their coming all his life. Several Rebel cavalrymen had deceived them after Atlanta, pretending to be Northerners, to expose slave sympathies. When they expressed en-thusiasm for being freed, they were flogged.* Pointing toward the trackage of the Atlanta & Augusta Railroad, which had been destroyed, he said, "In dat ar woods over dar is buried eber so many black men who were killed, sar, yes, killed a working on dat road—whipped to death. I seed 'em, sar."

One of the staff offered the old man a drink. The whiskey further "set his tongue going." Hearing him, Lieutenant David R. Snelling, a lanky native Georgian of twenty-six in Sherman's escort, recognized, Hitchcock wrote,

> a favorite slave of his uncle, who resided about six miles off; but the old slave did not at first recognize his young master in our uniform. One of my staff-officers asked him what had become of his young master. . . . He did not know, only that he had gone off to the war, and he supposed him killed, as a matter of course. His attention was then drawn to Snelling's face, when he fell on his knees and thanked God that he had found his young master alive and along with the Yankees. Snelling inquired all about his uncle and the family, asked my permission to go and pay his uncle a visit, which I granted, of course. . . . The uncle was not cordial, by any means, to find his nephew in the ranks of the host that was desolating the land, and Snelling came back, having exchanged his tired horse for a fresher one out of his uncle's stables, explaining that surely some of the "bummers" would have got the horse had he not.

---

* Sherman's memoirs, written some years after the occurence, quote the slave somewhat differently than Hitchcock does in his diary. The more immediate recollection is used here.

Snelling confided to Hitchcock that early in the rebellion, when he planned to hide in the woods until he could escape north to join the Federals, and asked his uncle, David Lester, for a blanket, Lester grew suspicious and refused. Still, Snelling paid his family visit, Lester grumbling to his renegade nephew that Sherman was "the greatest general and the meanest man in the world." Nursing his own grudge, Snelling would return to burn Lester's gin house.

Sending a courier to General Davis, Sherman explained that they were on one of Cobb's plantations, instructing him "to spare nothing." He exempted the wretched log slave huts through which the winds seeped, and sufficient provisions for the abandoned blacks. Sherman advised them that the Federals were their friends and they need not be afraid. "I s'pose dat you'se true," said an anxious old man, "but, massa, you'll go 'way tomorrow and anudder white man will come." His wife asked, as a drove of cattle passed, "whar' did all them beef come from?" Told that they came from Chicago, a thousand miles away, she exclaimed, "Lor', what a population you Yanks is!"

That night "the teamsters and men, as well as the slaves, carried off an immense quantity of corn and provisions of all sorts." Bonfires "consumed the fence-rails, [and] kept our soldiers warm."

PANIC HAD ARISEN in Milledgeville several days earlier. In the absence of the militia, other than a battery of artillery soon to bolt, and a company of "Factory Guards," ostensibly protecting the city were 160 teenage cadets from the burned-out Georgia Military Institute in Marietta, north of Atlanta. They had been moved from the path of the Federals during the summer, and drilled and tented on State House Square. To bolster the defenses, Governor Joseph Emerson Brown appealed to the patriotism of inmates in the state prison, offering pardons to all who accepted military service. Few of the prisoners refused. The 126 volunteers were ordered to load trains. Then militia adjutant general Henry C. Wayne, son of a Union Supreme Court justice, removed the boys, militiamen, and ex-convicts from Milledgeville and sent them eastward to guard a railroad bridge over the Oconee River at Ball's Ferry, nearby. With them were several hundred survivors of the 4th ("Orphan") Kentucky Brigade, whose veteran captain, John Weller, recalled seeing the hapless Wayne "arrayed in a brilliant uniform," with his staff around him "in fine style," commanding bewildered cadets and less-than-eager convicts.

Holding the bridge while vastly outnumbered soon seemed unprofitable. The Federals would be coming in force. The Kentuckians withdrew north, one laggard taking a wound and barely evading capture. Some of the convicts, still in prison uniforms, deserted and were taken prisoner. Sherman ordered them released, to create whatever trouble they could in areas his troops would leave. Wayne led the remainder to the Milledgeville depot, where his ineffectives boarded an oncoming Georgia Central Railroad train, on a spur southward toward Gordon and Macon.

The hasty exodus to Gordon, twenty miles south of Milledgeville, occurred just before General Howard's right wing began the rail line's systematic destruction. Just to the west was the town of Clinton, where two reporters with the Federals stopped for the night at the home of an elderly woman and identified themselves to her daughter, a youngish widow, as representatives of the *Cincinnati Commercial* and the *New York World*, which had supported McClellan. The Cincinnati correspondent was garbed in Union blue, which might have been off-putting, but the ladies sensed protection. "I'm so glad to meet you!" gushed the daughter hopefully. "It's seldom one gets a word of cheer these days. You'll stay until all the troops pass through—won't you?"

They dined in rare style, enjoyed the ladies' conversation, listened to the younger woman play the piano, and slept in real beds. The next morning at breakfast the New Yorker confessed that he could not deceive the ladies any longer: "Allow me to say that I am not a correspondent for the *New York World*, but for the *New York Tribune*, that great apostolic Abolition sheet."

"Oh, it can make no difference to us," the daughter said quickly, but when her mother wondered about the difference between the newspapers, as she had not heard of either, the younger woman said, "Why, Ma, don't you know that the *World* sympathizes with us!" Whether or not their feelings about the Union cause were in question, Southern hospitality had saved their house and possessions.

Had the ladies read any local papers, they would not have been reassured by the Georgia press. Unhelpfully, General Pierre Beauregard had telegraphed from two states away in Corinth, Mississippi, on the eighteenth:

> To the people of Georgia:
> Arise for the defense of your native soil! Rally around your patriotic Governor and gallant soldiers! Obstruct and destroy all the roads in Sherman's front, flank, and rear, and his army will soon starve in your midst. Be confident. Be resolute. Trust in an overruling Providence, and success will soon crown your efforts. I hasten to join you in the defense of your homes and firesides.

Matching Beauregard's bravado, a Georgia senator wired from remote Richmond:

> You have now the best opportunity ever presented to destroy the enemy. Put every thing at the disposal of our generals; remove all provisions from the path of the invaders, and put all obstructions in his path. Every citizen with his gun, and every negro with his spade and axe, can do the work of a

soldier. You can destroy the enemy by retarding his march. Georgians, be firm, act promptly, and fear not!

Augusta and Macon were divided by Sherman's armies and effectively out of the fight. As one or both might be targets, "Fighting Joe" Wheeler wondered where to turn, other than to have his horsemen harass, to little effect, the Federal flanks. "Enemy turning column shortest route to Macon," he telegraphed higher authority. "I have no orders regarding the holding of any city should enemy besiege or assault. Please give me wishes and intentions of Government, or send someone who knows the course they desire pursued."

Secretary of War James Seddon and Lieutenant General Robert E. Lee had no idea how to resist Sherman, or where he was going, beyond the immediate target of Milledgeville. The *Richmond Examiner* quoted dispatches that the Federals were "marching rapidly on Macon and report his advance as having reached the outskirts of the city. They have no hope that Cobb's militia will be able to hold Macon." To furnish advice, Lee wired Richard Taylor, a bushy-mustached, brainy general based in Montgomery, Alabama, to rush by rail to Macon, where much of the Georgia leadership had gathered. Heredity and connections made Taylor, son of a Mexican War hero who had become president, something of an oracle.

The chief conferees were Major General Howell Cobb of the Georgia Militia; Robert Toombs, its inspector general and a former senator; and Major General Gustavus W. Smith of the Georgia Militia, who had left his position as New York's streets commissioner to defend his home state. Just arrived at local militia headquarters, until the week before a private home, was Governor Brown, a bitter political enemy of the patrician Howell Cobb, his predecessor, with whom he was not on speaking terms. Brown "gave me," Taylor would recall, "a laughable account of the expeditious manner in which he and his 'little party' got to Macon." As Taylor arrived, Brown was confidently composing "a superb dispatch to General Lee to inform him of the impossibility of Sherman's escape."

A brother-in-law of Jefferson Davis, Taylor was a rhetorically suave historian of military strategy and tactics who had studied at Harvard and Yale rather than West Point. He had commanded effectively in Virginia, Alabama, and Louisiana, where his splendid plantation, Fashion, with two hundred slaves inherited from his father, was sacked by Federals in 1862. "The ground was frozen and some snow was falling," Taylor recalled about Macon. Cobb had met him at the railway station in the chilly dawn and offered, "We'll ride out and see the defenses. I've been up all night working on them. The Yankees were only twelve miles away at noon yesterday."

Taylor declined. "There's no need to see the trenches, and I hope you'll stop your workmen and let all of them get warm by the fire—which is where I'm going to stay. Sherman's not coming here." Realizing that the Federals had come close, then drawn away, or they would already have been swarming over Macon, Taylor was sure that Sherman was not interested in the town. He recommended sending troops, urgently, somewhere else—like Savannah—before it was too late. Milledgeville was doomed, and very likely all of eastern Georgia. Like Governor Brown, the privileged population of the state capital—its officials and legislators and their families—had already taken a different train to Macon.

FOUR

Making Georgia Howl

O NCE THE LOCAL AUTHORITIES AWAKENED TO THE reality that despite Sherman's feints toward Augusta and Macon, Milledgeville was the immediate objective, the state legislature had been called into an unprecedented morning session to conscript every able-bodied Georgian not yet in uniform. The law exempted members of the judiciary and the legislature. It also struck back at President Davis, who proposed overriding states' rights to summon every male to Confederate service. Governor Brown, a popular maverick, wired "a most emphatic protest against the extraordinary recommendation," as it would "annihilate the last vestige of State Sovereignty"—a pillar of secession. Only three hundred Georgia regulars remained in the state, manning an offshore fort.

There was "much excitement," Anna Maria Green, daughter of Dr. Thomas A. Green, the director of the state asylum for the insane, wrote in her diary. With her father she went to the State House to observe the "truly ridiculous" scene. "The members were badly scared, . . . made my cheeks glow with shame." By voice vote, they authorized three thousand taxpayer dollars for a special train to deposit them, vaguely, at "the front, . . . to meet again if we should live, at such place as the Governor may designate."

After stripping the governor's columned mansion on Clark Street of its rugs, curtains, bedding, furniture, dishes, and silver, emptying the pantry and even putting a cow aboard a rail car for fresh milk, Brown led the exodus away from wherever Georgia politicians thought the front was. The governor's wife, children, two spinster sisters, and their house slaves had preceded him. According to a neighbor, Mrs. Brown, "pale and terror-stricken," feared that their home would be "burned over her head before morning."

Once Brown had left for Macon, a political rival, Ambrose R. Wright, absentee president of the Georgia Senate, proclaimed from Augusta that since Brown could not oversee the eastern portion of state if cut off by the Federals, he—Wright—would be acting governor east of the Oconee River at Milledgeville. He urged Georgians to drop all other pursuits and battle the bluecoats. Savannah lawyer and planter Charles C. Jones, Jr., a former mayor who became an artillery officer, backed Wright on grounds of Brown's "territorial disability," and a telegram from Jefferson Davis supported Wright's tenuous authority in his rump of Georgia.

Fleeing, legislators left the State House with papers on their desks, abandoned the library and state archives, the armory, and the arsenal. The Great Seal of Georgia was hastily buried under a house. Teamsters asked exorbitant sums to convey wagonloads of private citizens and their goods to safety.

Frightened by the glow on the western horizon at dark, more likely from thousands of campfires than from burning farms, Anna Maria Green heard, melodramatically in her account, "the sound of weeping and heart-rending cries" from nearby houses. "Many of the white women were using the spade and hoe burying their treasures, not gold or silver, but pieces of homespun jeans and factory-cloth, intended to be made up for soldiers, also home-knit socks, pieces of bacon, etc." The Greens themselves plunged barrels of sorghum syrup into the city reservoir, and Anna stuffed her jewelry into a bag concealed beneath her petticoats.

An Atlanta lady who had fled to Milledgeville, Miss A. C. Cooper, breathlessly recalled (or invented) some of the hysteria in anticipation of the Federals. "The excitement increased, we could neither eat nor sleep," she wrote. "Scouts were sent up this road, down that, across the country; everywhere the roads teemed with foam-flecked, hard-run horses bestrode by excited men." The horsemen would return exhausted, and "not dismounting, take food from the willing hands that would carry it out to them, then off again." In the confusion, "Dogs howled and yelped. Mules bayed. Negro drivers swore, while Negro girls giggled." However sensational in her memory, the unconcealed route of the march, miles long, soon left plumes of smoke from torched gins and mills and barns winding upward in the near distance.

Through reddish mud and the residue from freezing rain, Union cavalry entered to reconnoiter early on the twenty-second. The outlying trenches and earthworks were unmanned. The town was quiet. In the unusual cold, icicles hung from roofs and eaves. Rapping on doors, bluecoats inquired where the Rebels were, and no one seemed to know. When Kilpatrick's horsemen rode back to report that Milledgeville was undefended, some townspeople thought happily that the Federals were in retreat, but Captain William Duncan of General Howard's headquarters scouts, back on duty after escaping from prison camp, and riding with four escorts, returned. He was greeted on the streets by Mayor Boswell DeGraffenreid, who formally yielded the capital and asked that people and property be spared. Duncan accepted the surrender, and even the mayor's unexpected hospitality, taking a glass of wine with DeGraffenreid at his home on Wilkinson Street. Nevertheless, en route back to their bivouac, crossing Government Square, Duncan's men ungraciously burned the depot and railway cars at a siding and cut the telegraph lines.

Early that afternoon, eight days out, troops began moving into Milledgeville. Sherman ordered Slocum's left wing to camp largely on the outskirts, on the banks of the Oconee River, as the entire force would overwhelm the town and offer temptation for looting and destruction. The *Savannah Daily News* had already reported in an imaginative wire from Augusta dated the twenty-third that Milledgeville was taken and that "the State House, Governor's mansion, and penitentiary were burned."

"Passed groves of pine cut down for works and abatis, not used," Hitchcock noted of the felled tree redoubts and lack of resistance. "First act of drama well played, General," he complimented Sherman as they cantered into Milledgeville, the major riding his not-always-disciplined Button. "Yes, sir," Sherman answered from the saddle, "the first act is played."

The town was "prettily situated," Hitchcock wrote—"some very good dwellings, State House, arsenal, Governor's Mansion, all fine, also hotel, good large building." In parade formation along Greene Street, XX Corps unfurled the Stars and Stripes and bands played "Yankee Doodle" and "Battle Hymn of the Republic." As they passed the State House, perhaps to infuriate Georgians, troops broke into "Dixie" and "We'll Hang Jeff Davis on a Sour Apple Tree." Two regiments left the ranks to camp at Capitol Square; others crossed the Oconee Bridge to bivouac.

In the deep South, military bands were no longer playing on the field of combat, as earlier. Snare drummers once "beat the rally" to inspire troops rushing into action. Bands were still largely manned by fifers, buglers (or cornetists), and drummers; all musicians expected to perform other duties as needed. On rare occasions the war had even stopped momentarily for a performance. Flags of truce were usually employed for exchanging prisoners, burying the dead, or permitting civilians through the lines, but during the siege of Atlanta, according to Colonel James Nisbet of the 66th Georgia, one Rebel regiment showcased the best cornet player he had ever heard. "In the evenings after supper he would come to our salient and play solos." Sherman's troops were close enough to applaud. "They had a good cornet player who would"—very likely during a temporary truce—"alternate with our man."

Blacks who had clung to the marchers since Atlanta followed the troops, and the music. Unhindered, the local slave population poured out into the streets, some in their Sunday clothes. "Bress de Lord! Tanks be to Almighty God, the Yanks is come; de day of jubilee hab arrived!" one cried ecstatically, according to David Conyngham of the *New York Herald*. Another declared, "I can't stop laughing enough. I'm so glad to see you." A woman rushed out to hug several soldiers, announcing, "One of you's gotta marry me!" Anxious soldiers slipped into the middle of the ranks to evade the excesses of happiness.

With only his bedroll and saddlebags, Sherman moved briefly into the abandoned governor's mansion, where the few merchants remaining— they had stayed to protect their cotton—soon pleaded their case to him. The Confederacy, one allowed, was "played out." Although Sherman agreed to destroy no cotton under bond that assured it would not go to the Rebels, and ordered Hitchcock, his lawyer, to draw up appropriate papers, before that could be accomplished word came that 270 bales* had already been burned "not by order," and that General Slocum's guards sent to prevent such torching had arrived "too late. Too bad." An elderly cotton broker Hitchcock identified as Leopold Waitzfelder explained that although everyone he knew claimed to want peace, they also wanted to keep their slaves. It was too late for that, said Hitchcock.

In Milledgeville, Sherman turned up newspapers from across the

---

* 1,700, according to the *New York Herald*.

Confederacy "and learned of the consternation which had filled the Southern mind at our temerity; many charging that we were actually fleeing for our lives and seeking safety at the hands of our fleet on the sea-coast. . . . The outside world must have supposed us ruined and lost." Some papers included a report from Richmond signed by six Georgia members of the Rebel legislature announcing that they had held "a special conference with President Davis and the Secretary of War, and are able to assure you that they have done, and are still doing all that can be done to meet the emergency that presses on you." They urged that "every man fly to arms" and that citizens impede the Federals in every possible way. Perhaps in response, Sherman issued his intimidating Special Field Order No. 127 directing that civilians obstructing the march were to be dealt with "harshly." When food or forage was destroyed to keep it from the Federals, "houses, barns, and cotton gins must also be burned to keep them company."

As the general sat in the empty governor's mansion on the afternoon of November 23, using planks across two camp chairs for a desk, "Some of the officers (in the spirit of mischief)," he recalled (they were largely from the 34th Wisconsin and 107th New York regiments), "gathered together in the vacant, vandalized Hall of Representatives, elected a Speaker, and constituted themselves the Legislature of the State of Georgia! A proposition was made to repeal the ordinance of secession, which was well debated, and resulted in its repeal by a fair vote!" One participant was the inebriated Hugh Judson Kilpatrick, who raised a bottle of plundered brandy and gibed that he had "come so far to visit the good people of Georgia, who are famed for their hospitality. . . ." Several officers crawled under their desks, feigning "bourbon fits" legendary among Southern legislators. An article jokingly repealing secession read, "As the Federal relations with the state are not very friendly, that a committee be appointed to kick Joe Brown and Jeff Davis, and also to whip back the state into the Union." The committee, authorized by voice vote, was

Sherman's entire army. The general "enjoyed the joke," although Hitchcock deplored the mockery: "I was named to draw up resolutions, etc., but was luckily busy drawing bond[s] for cotton, etc. Glad of it."

Hitchcock also read a report from General Howard that noted "with outrage" breaches of discipline in his right wing, now close to the upper column. Hitchcock had regularly written of excesses in his diary, while conceding, "Certainly an army is a terrible engine and hard to control." He blamed "J.D. & Co." as responsible for creating, by rebellion, the monster that war was. Although the New York Herald would claim in a dispatch filed later "no instance of pillage or insult to the inhabitants," Anna Maria Green wrote of an unreported rape. Kate Latimer Nichols, wife of a Confederate captain on duty in Virginia, had been ill and bedridden in a farmhouse on the outskirts of Milledgeville, alone but for her slaves, one of whom guarded her door. At gunpoint, two Union soldiers pushed him aside, broke in, and forced themselves on Mrs. Nichols. "Poor woman," Miss Green wrote on hearing of the attack, "I fear that she has been driven crazy." Kate Nichols, then twenty-seven, died, insane, soon after the war.

Reports of sexual attacks were common, but rarely proved. A woman shamed by the episode would be reluctant to confess it. A claim in a Savannah paper on December 6 that "some of the nicest ladies in Milledgeville" were "ravished" was an exaggeration of the Kate Nichols case, and many allegations about rapes of young black women were made by angry slavers whose human property had absconded with the Federals. The Richmond Dispatch on December 7 went even further about heartless "violence toward the ladies. At least six or seven suffered the last extremity. One young girl became crazed in consequence, and has been sent to the asylum. Other ladies were stripped of their garments, and, in such a plight, compelled to play the piano; and in the event of a refusal, switched unmercifully. Let Georgians remember these things in the day of battle!" Rather than rouse Georgians on the Virginia front to fight harder, the inventions may have led to increased desertions—defending the honor of threatened womenfolk at home.

In one military justice case, the court martial of Private John Bass found him guilty of attempted rape, although he had only brandished a revolver at a woman who called him a "Nigger stealer." Bass's head was shaved, and he was ordered to be dishonorably discharged as soon as it became practical to release him. General Howard explained to the soldier's irate commanding officer that it was necessary to "make an example of someone and just as well a 48th [Illinois] man as anyone else."

Although Milledgeville escaped rather lightly, there was also authorized violence. The armory was blown up after a cache of unusable Revolutionary War weapons was confiscated—muskets, pistols, and shotguns. Some soldiers appropriated the relics, as well as crude blades intended for improvised pikes, as premature Christmas presents to themselves. A Federal observing the removal of the implements remarked, "It is one of old Joe Brown's ideas, and like him has vanished." (When enlistees had lacked rifles with bayonets, the governor had ordered them to shoulder the "Georgia pike," an eighteen-inch blade fixed into a six-foot staff.) Explosives, and six wagonloads of useless weapons, were dumped into the Oconee. Sherman also ordered the destruction "of such public buildings as could easily be converted to hostile uses." Since convicts in the penitentiary had been manufacturing rifles and other arms, it was due for burning, but the twenty who had refused parole in exchange for emergency military service torched their cells in the chaos and escaped.

Sherman claimed mildly in his memoirs "little or no damage . . . done to private property, and General Slocum, with my approval, spared several mills, and many thousands of bales of cotton, taking what he knew to be worthless bonds, that the cotton should not be used for the Confederacy." Given how late in the day it was for the faltering rebellion, and the shortage of accessible harbors and trackage to ship bales abroad

THE PENITENTIARY AT MILLEDGEVILLE BURNS

through the Union blockade, Sherman felt that he could spare wholesale destruction.

"Little or no damage" also meant the torching of a few homes in Milledgeville, including those of the state treasurer, John Jones, and Judge Iverson Harris, who had urged townspeople to obstruct the Federals by any means. His was one of the first properties to be burned under Sherman's Field Order 127. Another casualty was the plantation of William A. Jarrett, after its overseer, Patrick Kane, fired at oncoming troops and was shot down—the only fatality during the occupation of Milledgeville. From his vandalized house on Columbia Street, Peterson Thweatt, Georgia's comptroller general, would complain to Confederate vice president Alexander Stephens, "All our provisions, crockery, silver, bed clothing, our own clothing . . . were taken or destroyed. Our parlor furniture given away to negroes. . . . Our nurse was taken and has never been heard from since. My wife and children lived on Potatoes for several days." A local woman whose home would be burned in reprisal vented her hatred by hurling a rock out of a second-story window at bluecoats below. Another in ladylike silks opened her front door, walked up to a passing Union column, and spit at a soldier. Troops left their ranks to fire her house.

The twenty-third was a Wednesday, with Thanksgiving Day to follow. Since most troops would break camp that Thursday, Wednesday evening as well as the official holiday became times for festivity. Camped behind slave quarters on an otherwise abandoned plantation, Private Rice Bull and his New Yorkers found what he described as a thousand bushels of buried sweet potatoes, which soon vanished into XX Corps dinners. "A party of us boys"—ten of them—found an "old Negro aunty" in a cabin and offered her two Union dollars to make them a Thanksgiving feast. With the sweet potatoes they brought several hens, a goose, some fresh pork, a bag of wheat flour, and coffee. For "Aunt Susan," who was "big, fat, and black as tar," they cleaned the fowls, carried in water, and stoked the fire. She baked biscuits in an iron Dutch oven and fricasseed the meat, which went into a large pot with the potatoes. "We had all we could eat. I do not believe there were many homes in the North who had their Thanksgiving Dinner . . . who were more thankful than we were in the Negro hut in Milledgeville."

At six in the evening Private Bull and the other men gathered their belongings to return to camp, leaving much of the uneaten feast to "Aunt Susan," and bade her goodbye. After the warm cabin, tenting in the frost was difficult, but "the memory of that meal lingered long."

Campfires had sprung up all over the Milledgeville area, some fed with burning pews removed from churches in State House Square. Attracted by the glow, several emaciated, hollow-cheeked men in rags emerged from the darkness, escapees from the infamous prison pen at Andersonville, a hundred miles to the south. They had evaded search parties and bloodhounds, wept at the sight of the Union flag, and gazed with "wild animal stares" at the roasting beef, pork, and poultry being prepared by Colonel Charles D. Kerr's 16th Illinois, whose troops, he noted, were "sickened and infuriated" by the evidence of gross mistreatment. All about lower Georgia, they realized, were barns bursting with grain and fields tall with corn.

Private Amos Stearns of the 25th Massachusetts, a prisoner at Andersonville who did not make it out, wrote in his diary, "Today is Thanksgiving Day at home, I suppose, and no doubt the folks there are thinking of me and saying they wished he was here and I wish I was there. . . . Rations today of meal & salt. They have cut down our rations." But there were three issues rather than two, the others largely beans and rice—"and I was thankful for all this even."

The correspondent of the *Cincinnati Gazette* claimed, once Sherman's communications were restored, that bloodhounds were "kept at all guard stations and picket-posts throughout the South . . . for the purpose of hunting escaped prisoners and rebel deserters," and that in one incident a New York soldier, two from Illinois, and a boy prisoner of unidentified origin were recaptured and thrown to the dogs.* An Andersonville escapee named Crummel was beaten with a musket, after which twenty Rebels formed a ring and let the bloodhounds at him. "He was terribly torn, and soon after died. Harris and Cloes were treated in the same way. . . . Patterson, who was a mere boy, kneeled down and prayed." He was kicked in the head, knocking out his front teeth, and thrown in the ring, but the dogs "had satiated themselves with blood, and refused to touch him." Then abandoned, he found his way to Sherman's marchers and told his tale.

More reports of brutality came from Kilpatrick, who alleged to Hitchcock that his strayed horsemen taken captive by Wheeler's cavalry near Macon had been threatened with death if they did not take oaths of

---

* A Milwaukee newspaper reported in January 1865, based on allegations from the surgeon of the 14th Wisconsin, that bloodhounds found on the march were "slaughtered without mercy, not far from five hundred being killed daily." The number seems absurd.

allegiance to the Confederacy. Four did. Others were murdered. Two left to die were retrieved alive because "Rebs had sliced their throats too far up."

"If this proves true," Hitchcock wrote, "Sherman will retaliate, *and we must not be taken prisoners*. I confess I don't expect any mercy if captured: and the worst of it is that the 'foraging' or pillaging by our men is bound to bring this about. It is all wrong. Certainly the laws of war allow of damage enough being done to teach a terrible lesson, and that lesson must be taught: it is unavoidable and right. But I would find a way to stop anything beyond." Colonel William Hawley of the XX Corps' 3rd Wisconsin Volunteers recommended burning down the State House. Hitchcock objected, successfully, but he could not prevent the trashing of the interior, the smashing of windows, and the blackening of walls— including those of the lone hotel—with tobacco spittle. (Fifteen hundred pounds of tobacco warehoused in the town had been distributed to bluecoats.) Troops scooped up as souvenirs wads of Georgia paper currency, as did E. D. Westfall of the *New York Herald* and Associated Press, who wrote to the *Herald* in a dispatch he could not yet post, "Being rather short of decent paper on which to write this communication, I have the honor to forward it to you on the back of the rebel 'grayback notes.' I have been somewhat surprised to find that I have used up over a million dollars in this with my task only half finished. I have plenty, however."

"THIS IS THANKSGIVING DAY at home," Hitchcock began his diary on November 24. "God hasten the day when we shall all unite, North and South, East and West, in heartfelt thanksgiving for Peace and Victory over these accursed rebel leaders!" With Sherman, he broke camp at ten in the morning, riding with the lead elements of XX Corps. But for abandoned rubbish, the governor's mansion was left as empty as they had found it. The armies of Slocum and Howard had converged east of Milledgeville, and now would separate again. The bridge across the Oconee had been left undestroyed by Harry Wayne's improvised defenders, and was traversed easily, but the Federals turned back many of the blacks who tried to follow them and impede progress. Only one persistent young slave, Allen Brantley, having proved his efficiency, was kept as a teamster. He would remain in service through the war and earned an army pension.

Later in the march, troops would pick up a Savannah paper dated December 5, which quoted a letter from Milledgeville alleging that while in the city, the Federals hosted a grand ball at which only black and mulatto women were present, the white women indignantly refusing to attend. It was the first that anyone in Sherman's army had heard of it. According to Major John Chipman Gray, General Howard was "much disgusted by a story in the rebel papers, that at a ball in Macon he led off the first dance with a negro woman." (The Federals never occupied Macon.) Also, reportedly, one of the few women convicts in the abandoned penitentiary in Milledgeville was slipped into the campsite of the 33rd Indiana concealed in a Federal uniform and plied her former trade before the regiment broke camp.

THE SKY WAS BLUE, and the air eastward from Milledgeville was bracing. The steep hills leading into dense groves of pines were heavy going for the loaded wagons and lowing cattle. Although Georgians along the route, and those threatened by foragers and bummers on either side for miles, lived in terror of the Federals, David Conyngham of the *New York Herald* made their almost unopposed progress seem idyllic for his Northern readers. "All day long," he wrote,

> the army has been moving through magnificent pine woods—
> the savannahs of the South, as they are termed. I have never

MOST SHOOTING DONE BY UNION TROOPS WAS FOR
KILLING PIGS, CATTLE, AND OTHER ANIMALS FOR FOOD

seen, and I can't conceive a more picturesque sight than the
army winding along through these grand old woods. The pines
rise naked of branches, eighty and ninety feet, and then are
crowned with a tuft of pure green. The trees are wide apart,
so that frequently two trains of wagons and troops in double
column are marching abreast. In the distance may be seen a
troop of horsemen, and some general and his staff, turning
about here and there, their gay uniforms, and red and white
flags contrasting harmoniously with the bright, yellow grass
underneath and the deep evergreen. War has its romance and
its pleasures, and nothing could be more delightful, nor can

there be more beautiful subjects for the artist's pencil than a thousand sights which have met my eye for days past, and which can never be seen outside the army.

Riding ahead was Major Lewis M. Dayton, Sherman's aide-de-camp, and his party. Their assignment was to pick a place to bed down the column for the night that would be far enough along to include space to the rear for the mule-drawn supply train, four hours and thirteen miles behind, to catch up. For the general, Dayton found a house near Gum Creek occupied by a widowed lady of sixty-five and her fat, and frightened, spinster daughter, who confessed, "I shall sleep a lot better tonight than last night—they said you would all burn our house over our heads—kept me awake all night." Discovering that Dr. John Moore, Sherman's staff surgeon, was unmarried, the elder lady heaped praise on her daughter's domestic skills: "powerful fast knitter—could keep a bachelor's ankles mighty warm." She asked innocently whether the Federals had brought any "pi-anners" with them, as her daughter "could play mighty well."

Some Federals remained near Milledgeville through Thanksgiving Day to round up stragglers and to protect the rear of the wagon train. In choosing a campsite, scouts gave preference to slopes for drainage and visibility, and to proximity to wood and water. The leading division would pitch tents first; those in the rear would halt farther ahead, becoming the lead units the next morning. After stacking arms, troops would cut wood, park wagons, and corral and feed animals. At their campfires early in the march, David Conyngham wrote, the troops scorned chickens "in the plenitude of turkeys with which they have supplied themselves. Vegetables of all kinds and in unlimited quantities were at hand, and the soldiers gave thanks as soldiers may, and were merry as soldiers can be. In truth, as far as the gratification of the stomach goes, the troops are pursuing a continuous thanksgiving."

A bugler would sound out a closing "Go to rest, go to rest," his tat-too, according to Major Nichols, "as plain as organs of human speech." Soon "Taps" would follow—"Out lights; out lights; out lights." While snow squalls still blew across the riverbank east of Milledgeville, chilled soldiers wound into their blankets and campfires flickered down.

Breaking camp in darkness was uncomfortable but disciplined. At the open ends of tents, embers had burned low by reveille. The order of march went down the line squad by squad, as in "The second division will be on the Milledgeville road promptly at five o'clock." In Conyngham's description, "Fires spring up again to fry potatoes and bacon; chicken roasts; coffee pots steam. Horses and mules are given fodder, and bray, neigh, snuffle and paw. Then the fires are smothered, animals hitched or led, knapsacks strapped, and weapons recovered."

On the morning of November 25, the Friday after Thanksgiving, kin-dling piled at both ends of the wooden span over the Oconee was torched while the toll taker, his occupation gone, watched helplessly. Major James Connolly, commanding the rear guard, left behind the "fat, dirty, lazy-looking citizen," looking on "with a woeful countenance as he beheld us fire the bridge." As Connolly crossed with the last of his Illinois regiment, the unhappy toll man assured the major that he had "allers bin for the Union, and wus yit." In ten minutes the span collapsed, delaying harass-ment from Rebel horsemen somewhere to the rear.

"THIS MORNING through the spy glass," Anna Maria Green wrote, "we watched the burning of the bridge after the retreating enemy, and after-wards stood and hailed the entrance of our beloved soldiers amid shouts and tears." Somehow, she misinterpreted the unhindered departure of the Federals eastward, bands playing and flags flying, as a retreat, and the cautious entrance into the suddenly empty streets of a small band of Confederate horsemen, who had prudently remained distant, as a

Rebel victory. They were Wheeler's scouts, approaching to survey what was left of Milledgeville. "A few ragged men came riding up," she wrote, "and bowed and brandished their pistols; the tears streamed from our eyes—strong men wept." Although the cliché attracted her, there were no strong men left in Milledgeville.

That Saturday the Greens offered breakfast to a soldier who had come to seek tow rope for crude rafts across the Oconee near the debris of the burned bridge. Cavalrymen were already "swimming the horses." Three more scouts breakfasted with the Greens, one—a Kentuckian detached from the "Orphan Brigade"—was "almost barefoot." Harriet, their black maid (Anderson, a male slave, "had left with the Yankees"—to suffer, Anna was sure), "took off the new shoes Aunty had given her a few days before and offered them, saying she could do better without them than he could. If the Yankees knew of that little incident of one of our Negroes doing that kindness to a soldier and because he was a Confederate soldier, they might feel a little less kindly to our servants than they pretend." His foot size was apparently small.

Despite scattered vandalism, mostly within public buildings, the Georgia capital survived. Churches around the state house square had suffered some damage from the explosion of the arsenal and loss of some pews, but held Sunday services. Littered state documents were retrieved from streets and yards; looted books from the state library in the basement of the capital building and unburned, but wet from exposure to rain and frost, were recovered from local fields.

The revived *Milledgeville Confederate-Union* contended two weeks later, "A full detail of all the enormities . . . would fill a volume, and some of them would be too bad to publish. In short, if an Army of Devils, just let loose from the bottomless pit, were to invade the city, they could not be much worse than Sherman's army." The *Richmond Whig* claimed, "The visit of the Yankees to Milledgeville has worked a wonderful change. As the *Confederate Union* says, 'All reconstructionists and tepid war men have become the hot advocates of an everlasting strife, rather than submission or compromise. . . .'"

Mayor DeGraffenreid sent a courier south to Macon to plead for assistance. "Our citizens," he claimed, "have been utterly despoiled by the Yankee army. Send us bread and meat, or there will be great suffering among us. We have no mules or horses. What you send must be brought by wagon trains." Howell Cobb ordered the Confederate commissary to send a token five thousand rations of corn meal and eighteen head of beef. Alexander Collie, a London businessman operating from Macon who had profited handsomely in running cotton through the Union blockade, and helped finance the Southern Independence Association in England, donated $5,000 for Milledgeville relief.

While the Federals camped at Milledgeville, Richard Taylor commandeered his way to Savannah via Thomasville, on a railway engine and lone freight car. At about midnight General Hardee, officially commander of the Department of South Carolina, Georgia, and Florida, but holed up in Savannah, met him at the platform. Hardee was still in telegraph contact, in some cases circuitously, with other Confederate locations. Having pooled their intelligence into the morning, they estimated shrewdly but gloomily what lay in jeopardy by Christmas and what just seemed spared. To General Lee in Richmond, Taylor wired that

> Augusta, held by General [Braxton] Bragg with a limited force, was no longer threatened, as the enemy had passed south of it. Sherman, with sixty or seventy thousand men, was moving on the high ground between the Savannah and the Ogeechee Rivers; and as this afforded a dry, sandy road direct to Savannah, where he would meet most readily the Federal fleet, it was probable that he would adhere to it. He might cross the Savannah river forty or fifty miles above and march on Charleston, but this was hardly to be expected;

for . . . his desire to communicate with the fleet by the nearest route and in the shortest time must be considered. Hardee's force was inadequate to the defense of Savannah, and he should prepare to abandon the place before he was shut up. Uniting, Bragg and Hardee should call in the garrison from Charleston, and all scattered forces along the coast south of Wilmington, North Carolina, and be prepared to resist Sherman's march through the Carolinas, which he must be expected to undertake as soon as he had established a base on the ocean.

Hardee read and grimly approved the report. But for failing to anticipate how foul weather in late autumn would slow Sherman's advance west of Savannah, Taylor had penetrated the general's thinking and posited the best of what were only poor solutions. Two days later he slipped out, returning via Andersonville, where prison conditions appalled him. He endorsed the commandant's renewed but ignored appeals for food and blankets, found a train there traveling hazardously north to Meridian and thence to the Tennessee border, meeting there on orders from Lee with a whipped General Hood. Weeks later, Taylor was back in strategically unimportant Alabama via the marginally operational Mobile and Ohio.

As SHERMAN CONTINUED EASTWARD with XX Corps, Judson Kilpatrick's cavalrymen feinted toward Augusta, to the northeast, to entice possible Confederate reinforcements away from Savannah. As a preliminary, "Lil' Kil" had officers weed out the weakest horses, as a surplus had already been seized. Brutally, he ordered their heads hooded by blankets, and each horse killed by ax blows, then left to decay in the field. "My God!" cried the farmer, confronting the carnage, "I'll have to move!"

Kilpatrick's actual goal was Millen, more to the east, where Sherman thought Union prisoners were still held. Before the Federals could cut the rail lines, however, the weak and debilitated POWs had already been herded aboard flatcars and relocated.

After the first daily halt to rest, Sherman's escort overtook General John Geary's Second Division of Ohio, New York, New Jersey, and Pennsylvania infantrymen. A house close to their route, occupied by an elderly lady, Mrs. Greer, was found for Sherman. With her livestock gone, she mourned to his staff that she had lost everything, but her daughter cautiously suggested that the "gentlemen" were not responsible for their plight. Hitchcock and Nichols pitched their tent in the yard and built a blaze of fallen branches, its light sufficient for penciling Hitchcock's daily diary of the ninth day out. "Across the road directly in front of [the] house, is pine forest, dense shadows, sombre growth. General Slocum's tents are pitched across the road; and one division camps all around us: camp fires light up the open sky in rear of house: horses picketed in yard: sentry pacing before fence. . . . Camp sounds all round—voices in conversation in other tents—braying of mule[s] now and then, lowing of cattle, occasional shouts of soldiers." The droves of cattle to their rear were now "larger than when we left Atlanta."

"What road will you all go in the morning?" Mrs. Greer asked, curious as to where the column was heading.

"Really, Madam," Hitchcock explained on Sherman's behalf, "I suppose we'll have to go on the road *that runs by your house*—I see no other."

INTEREST WAS GREAT across both North and South in Sherman's future direction. On November 19, the *Chicago Tribune* asked, "Where is Sherman?" and the next day, unprompted from Chicago, the *New York Tribune* headlined, "Where has Sherman Gone?" Lincoln again got into the act, asking Alexander K. McClure if he would like to know where

Sherman was, and the chairman of the Republican Party in Pennsylvania took the bait. He certainly would, McClure conceded. "Well," said the President, "I'll be hanged if I wouldn't myself."

Although the Federals destroyed telegraph lines and railroad trackage as they encountered them, the worrying news of Sherman's whereabouts traveled, nevertheless, rapidly through the South. In the Roanoke Valley astride the North Carolina–Virginia border, Mrs. Catherine Edmondston wrote, after a gathering of nearby family on the twenty-fifth, "Sherman's move [is] the engrossing subject. Where is he going? He has sent out detachments in so many directions who have carried fire & sword with them that it is hard to discover the situation of his main body. He leaves a waste behind him. . . . As his intentions cannot be verified, speculation here is useless, but my heart bleeds for the poor people not only along his route but along his various threatened routes. What terrible suffering do one & what heart sickening suspense do the others endure? God be with them & give them the fruition of His promise."

NATHAN MORSE, the *Augusta Chronicle*'s editor, predicted that the Federals would bypass both Augusta and Savannah. The feints north and south were puzzling. Sherman might turn south toward Brunswick, he wrote, near the coastal border with Florida, or north toward Beaufort, South Carolina: "Although the Northern press has hinted that Sherman might attempt to march to Charleston by way of Augusta, recent developments we think show very clearly that such is not his design. If this were his route, he would not be diverging from it." The *Chronicle* also reported a litany of bummer excesses—farms that were "perfect wrecks," horses by the hundreds "lying dead," negroes (never "slaves") "gone," and, quoting the imaginative *Richmond Dispatch* rather than local sources, "700 prisoners" reaching Augusta, "having been captured while foraging for Sherman."

In its own guessing, the *Columbus Daily Times* punned with close knowledge of Georgia soil that "favorable *grounds* . . . exist for checking the advance of Sherman towards Savannah—grounds soft and moist." There were miles of marshlands ahead between Sherman and the coast. In a later editorial the *Times* noted, confidently, "Sherman has many days hard marching before . . . he will be able to respond visibly to the rockets of his friends on the coast, with a good prospect of having to fight his way through the entire distance." Vessels of the Union navy had been sighted off Wilmington, North Carolina, apparently steaming southward to reinforce captured Atlantic forts on the coast below, and by signal flares to announce the position of supply ships for Sherman, should he come close enough to see them.

The *Augusta Constitutionalist* was certain that Sherman's armies were marching toward their inevitable destruction in the palmetto swamps. "The hand of God is in it. The blow, if we can give it as it should be given, may end the war. Sherman has many weary miles to march. . . . It is an absurdity to talk about his making a winter campaign with no communication with his Government. He is retreating—simply retreating."

FIVE

Left Wing/Right Wing

O N THE DAY AFTER THE NORTHERN THANKSGIV-
ing, Malinda Taylor wrote encouragingly to her
husband from their Alabama farm, "We all eat a
very harty breakfast this morning. One month from today
is Christmas. God grant you may bee at home to spend one
more Christmas with me. The baby can sit alone [and] can
take any thing in his hand and grabs olde tom [the cat] when
he comes in his way." Private Grant Taylor of the 40th Alabama, gaunt and thirty-four, was safely garrisoned now on the
gulf coast. He had survived both pneumonia and Sherman's
thrust to Atlanta, after which he had written home, "Oh how
tired I am getting of this thing." However much it was a rich
man's war for the South, it was a poor man's fight. Malinda
had to butcher their only shoat for food, but had not "killed
my beef." She had been given a large rabbit caught by a wood-
cutter to cook, and the family had gone through only ten
bushels of their potatoes. Mrs. Taylor was sure that she would

get through what remained of the year without having to do in a cow, and was "so fat," she assured her husband, "my clothes will hardley meet on me." He would respond that she should lay in some beef: "It is useless to try to keep much stock on hand for if [you] winter them the government or the soldiers would take them from you."

That morning at dawn, as Sherman left Mrs. Greer's house, he asked Colonel Charles Ewing, his brother-in-law, who commanded Illinois and Wisconsin infantry nearby, to give the lady fifty dollars in Confederate currency—for her trouble and to compensate for the forage taken. Handing her daughter ("eighteen or nineteen, good rebel") five dollars on his own, Hitchcock was rebuked that the Union "had no right to punish helpless women who had never done anything." He asked where all her young friends had gone. "In the army," she said. "You have or had influence with them—did you ever use it," Hitchcock asked, "to keep them at home?" If they hadn't gone, she countered scornfully, they would have been called cowards. Other defiant, tight-lipped women, asked why they had let their husbands go off to an unwinnable war, told Federals bluntly that their men would have had no wives if they didn't. Captain Henry Heaton of the 2nd Iowa, in Howard's right wing, recalled that "in passing a poor shack of a house . . . , a woman and several little boys came out to look at us, and someone asked her if she did not think we would soon end the war. She said, 'Our men will fight you as long as they live, and then these boys will fight you when they grow up.'"

PROGRESS TOWARD SANDERSVILLE was halted as a burned crossing over swampy Buffalo Creek was repaired by Poe's engineers. As Sherman's staff watched from the grounds of an abandoned two-story frame house, blacks came forward from the farm's outbuildings, alleging that, before leaving, their owner had wrecked the bridge. Ewing offered to torch the house in retaliation. When Hitchcock contended that no evidence of guilt existed, Sherman, overhearing but unobserved ("nothing escapes him"), broke in, "In war everything is right which prevents anything. If bridges are burned, I have a right to burn all the houses near it. . . . Let him look to his own people." The slave huts remained, but Hitchcock knew he had lost the argument. War was war.

Since Sherman's war was also predicated upon foraging, authorized and otherwise, a private in the 113th Ohio would parody the general's order with facetious "rules," including:

> No [forage] detail shall be made to exceed the whole effective force, including negroes.

> No soldier will be allowed to take any horses or mules that cannot walk.

> No soldier shall carry off a grindstone weighing more than five hundred pounds.

> Burning of property is strictly prohibited, unless accidental, and any soldier caught attempting to fire any incombustible material will be arrested.

> Foraging will be conducted with as little shooting as possible, and no soldier will be allowed to shoot anything already dead.

Except for cultivated clearings, the land eastward was becoming too poor and thick with pines for useful foraging. "Strangers traveling through these woods," Major Connolly wrote, "will get lost as readily as on a prairie if they go too far from the road." They passed "miserable looking" little cabins, about which were "two or three sickly, sallow women and from five to fifteen children all looking like persons I have read of called 'dirt eaters'. . . . I think they must live on it, for I don't see a place for anything except children to grow. . . . " The culture of abject white poverty was new to Northerners, who expected only lush plantations and a slave-supported aristocracy; yet most families in the South, whatever their moral convictions, could not afford slaves. A black on a prosperous plantation told the *New York Herald*'s David Conyngham proudly, "White man no count here: dis nigger worth fifteen hundred dollars, white man nothing." Some poor whites were so impoverished and ignorant that Brigadier General W. B. Hazen, according to his memoirs, encountered one family that did not even know of the war.

NEAR SANDERSVILLE, other soldiers found further evidence of a subterranean class. An eighteen-year-old captain, Charles E. Belknap of the 21st Michigan,* leading a squad of foragers "after everything of foot and wing," came upon a lonely, mud-chinked log cabin that seemed deserted. Two "wee bits of girls," perhaps three and five years old, were in the single dark room. In the poor light, their grimy condition, and their crude dresses fashioned from burlap sacks with armholes, led Belknap to think that they were abandoned "darky" children. "Mamma gone, Mamma gone," explained one. Although they were "as shy as young partridges," the soldiers built a fire, heated some "soldiers' grub," and induced the children to be bathed and to let their hair be combed. Then the bluecoats scoured the area for other cabins, and asked the inhabitants if they knew the parents or were willing to take the girls in. Suspicious at best, the women would respond with variations of "I've got a houseful of my own."

Rather than abandon the children, Belknap's bummers stole cloth-

---

* In Grand Rapids, Belknap had enlisted at fifteen as a private. In Virginia and Tennessee, during the battles at Chickamauga and Stones River, he had been wounded seven times and received field promotions.

ing for the girls, threw their burlap sacks away, and "a soldier who had babies of his own in Michigan" dressed them. Riding on pack mules, they traveled with the troops and, in camp with the regiment at night, each slept nestled in a soldier's arms. They would celebrate Christmas in Savannah.

It was not Belknap's first brush with dirt-poor Southern whites. Closing in on Atlanta, his regiment reached Roswell, a busy textile town on the Chatahoochee River where rough barracks, he recalled, sheltered hundreds of half-starved "girls and women operatives" abandoned by

SOLDIERS WRECK THE IMPOSING RAILROAD
BRIDGE OVER THE OGEECHEE RIVER

fleeing factory managers. When Federals torched the mill, its walls held together with "cheap pitch" were soon "roaring" with flames. In terror, and with nowhere to go, the mill girls fled toward the river. Feeling at first that "it would be no loss to the army if some of them did sink," Belknap watched them go. Then, appalled, from his saddle on his horse, Dan, he ordered soldiers to each take one of the women on horseback across the shallow Chatahoochee. Once on the Marietta side, he arranged for those who wanted to return to the Confederate lines to do so on covered wagons under a flag of truce. The others were sent to safety on freight cars to Tennessee.

ON THE FAR SIDE OF THE OCONEE, troops exchanged shots with a reconnaissance party of Wheeler's horsemen, then stopped short of Sandersville with the two wings still nearly abreast of each other. With the right wing, Sherman rode with Major General Francis Blair's XVII Corps, Howard's XV Corps remaining to the outside, guarding the southern flank of the army. Above Sandersville, Slocum's wing was destroying trackage and telegraph lines as far as the next major crossing, the Ogeechee River. With the columns were Captain John C. Van Duzer and his fellow telegraph operators, who would tap into the wires to listen to Confederate wire traffic before breaking contact.

With transatlantic telegraphy still interrupted—the undersea cable to Ireland had operated only briefly in 1857 before splitting—Britain received its war news late, from steam packets that docked with the latest newspapers. Since the influential *Times* of London, still tenaciously pro-South, preferred dispatches from Richmond with an optimistic gloss on events, it continued to predict disaster for Sherman, who was allegedly "in difficulties." With Wheeler's cavalry harassing the Federals, yet only a pinprick in its progress, *The Times* editorialized on December 7, about ten days after its Southern spin on the realities:

It will be strange, indeed, if the army of General Sherman should arrive before Savannah, after such a march conducted under such difficulties, in condition to attack and storm a town so well fortified and so strenuously defended; and, if not, it is difficult to conceive a more embarrassing position than which General Sherman will occupy, with a wasted and weary army, a strong town at his front, and an army fighting on its own ground in his rear. We do not say that Sherman will not overcome all these obstacles. Any one of a hundred contingencies of which we have no knowledge may overthrow all our calculations, but arguing from the usual result of similar enterprises, from the well recognised principles of the military art, and from the spirit which the South has never failed to show, we cannot see the grounds for that tone of overweening confidence with which the Northern press hails the commencement of an expedition so novel and so hazardous, in which a General abandons one base of communications without, so far as we can see, any very clear or definite idea where he is to find another.

The Times guessed accurately at Sherman's destination. In his rear, however, he had left a ravaged land and tattered and vastly outnumbered pursuers who could not easily live on it, nor catch up in force, and he faced token troops who could not hold the Federals in check.

SANDERSVILLE, a town of about five hundred, was expected to be undefended, but some of Wheeler's scouts, guests at a home for dinner four miles west, had to remount hurriedly and flee, leaving two dead and several captured. Soon after, Wheeler himself, "a very small, very erect man"—he was five feet five—"wearing a crimson sash and a large black plumed hat, drew rein" and asked, at Ella Mitchell's house, about a skirmish "about four miles out." Ella's father knew about it. "Yes, General Wheeler," he said, "it is true," and he offered what he had heard from observers. Ella Mitchell, only nine, probably recalled what she knew as her ailing father told it. The black-bearded Wheeler, a major general at twenty-eight (bars and stars came early in armies short of competent leaders), was known by his flamboyant dress. Unafraid of being recognized, Wheeler was a born survivor, already wounded three times, with several horses shot from under him. Postwar, he would serve eight terms as a congressman and lead cavalrymen in Cuba during the Spanish-American War, retiring as a brigadier general under the flag he had opposed.

Wheeler slipped into Sandersville to surprise the first Federals. Breaking in, some of his men concealed themselves at upper windows of homes and behind porch pillars, with others on the courthouse portico. Surprised bluecoats ran for cover, returned fire, then withdrew. Hitchcock reported one dead, eleven captured. The outcome was worse. Union prisoners were put in an improvised holding pen in a shop. After dark, their guards were overpowered by a lynch mob, probably Rebel soldiers, who forced the captives into a nearby field and shot them. "At about three o'clock, Mr. [Pincus] Happ came in his carriage for father to go with him to bury the soldiers for the sake of humanity. Mother was afraid for father to go, he was so ill, but he went and took the two negro men servants we had. . . . Mr. Happ had his men. They buried the dead and returned before the day [broke]."

On the morning of November 27, a Saturday, Ella wrote, "We heard the firing of rifles and the yelling of men; then came a clattering of horses' hoofs, and a rain of bullets on the roof. Wheeler's men went dashing by, firing as they went. The road was a mass of blue men, the surrounding fields were full of them." After the Confederate escape, Sherman learned of the atrocity and ordered the town razed in reprisal. "Fences were torn down, hogs shot, cows butchered, women crying, children screaming. . . . Then the jail, the court house, peoples' barns and a large factory that made buckets and saddletrees, were all ablaze." The town's aged Methodist preacher, Brother Anthony, pleaded to have homes spared, contending that the killers were not local inhabitants, possibly not even Georgians. Hitchcock disparaged the minister as a "loud talker, vulgar fool"—but, relenting, Sherman said, "I don't war on women and children." Most residences would escape burning, but some had already been vandalized. "The ground was strewn with food, carpets were drenched with syrup and then covered with meal." Curiously, neither Sherman in his memoirs nor Hitchcock in his diaries mentions the prisoner murders.

Wheeler would keep turning up, even when he had not. On November 28, units of XV Corps foraged south into Johnson County but ventured too far off track toward tiny Wrightsville. Howard turned north to locate XVII Corps, leaving Tom Osborn, a major, to return troops to the march. In darkness, Osborn, on horseback, found a cabin where, seeking directions, he pretended, playing up his St. Louis accent, to be from Wheeler's cavalry. Wheeler was elsewhere. Riding away from Sandersville early that Saturday, he encountered the camp of Kilpatrick's cavalry, still under orders to search the prisoner of war compound at Millen. Absent when Wheeler raided the site, Kilpatrick and several staff officers were in a nearby cabin with two accommodating slave women, obviously absent without leave. Fleeing in surprise, "Kil" was nearly captured, losing only his trademark broad hat. (On another adventure he escaped in his underwear.) Some of his troops were taken, and fifty horses, along with blankets, overcoats, and prized battle flags. Regrouping his dismayed forces, twice the number of Wheeler's eighteen hundred men, Kilpatrick managed a fighting withdrawal toward a division in Slocum's column commanded by Brigadier General Absalom Baird. "I deemed it prudent to retire to our infantry," he explained.

"Confound the cavalry," a Union officer wrote on learning of the embarrassment. "They're good for nothing but to run down horses and steal chickens. I'd rather have one good regiment of infantry than the whole of Kilpatrick's cavalry." Reopening communications with the right wing, then abreast the Georgia Central route, General Carlin found Sherman sitting along a country lane, "wearing an old blue greatcoat. When I left the main column of Slocum's wing I understood that Wheeler had driven Kilpatrick back . . . and that Kilpatrick had called for a brigade of infantry to support him. General Sherman asked me the news . . . , and I told him." Surprised, Sherman said, "Why the fellow has just reported to me that he has whipped Wheeler!" Sherman would fudge the failure in his memoirs, where Kilpatrick "had considerable skirmishing" with Wheeler's cavalry but, "learning that our prisoners had been removed two days before from Millen, he returned . . . to the left wing." The episode, Sherman remarked, helpfully kept up "the delusion that the main army was moving toward Augusta."

MRS. NORA M. CANNING and her elderly husband, a retired judge, had left Macon for the safety of the family marshland plantation near the Ogeechee at Louisville. With growing concern they saw evidence of Kilpatrick's cavalry in the glow of burning cotton gins nearby. Still, she assumed that their twelve-mile distance from a railway line would keep them undisturbed. Their neighbor Herschel V. Johnson had no such illusions. He had been Stephen Douglas's vice presidential running mate in 1860, had declared that slavery "was safer in than out of the Union," and urged state militants not to follow South Carolina into secession. Retired to his plantation at Louisville, he called the course that Georgia took "the most stupendous blunder ever made by rational men," but when the legislature picked him for the Confederate Senate, he accepted the seat, changed his tune, and called "yielding" to the Federals "infamy." With

TREASURE SEEKERS SEARCH A PLANTATION

Sherman's march nearing Louisville, Johnson had his servants bury his silver and other household valuables in his garden under a bed of collard greens. Bummers who almost certainly had no idea whose property they were vandalizing, as everyone was the enemy, "found out the joke," as one explained.

Mrs. Canning and her servants had warily driven their livestock into a swamp and concealed their stocks of food, the hams under the floor of the smokehouse. For several days, Wheeler's men, in passing, would alert the family to the enemy's approach. Finally, at about noon on Monday, November 29, a slave boy came running to report that the Federals were coming down the lane: "Two white men's wid blue coats on." Soon there were "hundreds" to be seen. One asked Mrs. Canning at her door "how long it was since the last 'Rebs' had passed." When she remained silent, he demanded that she explain her refusal. "Don't you know," another soldier broke in, "the Southern women know no such persons as 'Rebs'?"

"I suppose," she answered feistily, according to her published memoirs, "that they are waiting for you down in the swamp." When they left, and she returned to her dining room, "The dishes were all gone, and even the table-cloth was taken."

The family was undisturbed at night, but the next morning a Confederate soldier came. He had been hiding in the woods and needed provisions and a place to hide. Soon the Federals returned, charging that a Rebel officer had been seen, and that he was somewhere in the house. They opened closets and cupboards, and "even the clock"—probably a tall grandfather clock. (It was dumped into a paddock.) "Sir," taunted the Rebel lady, to her cost, "there is one place you have not looked into"— and she pointed unhelpfully to a small pill box on the mantelpiece. "He turned away with a curse upon his lips on all the Rebel women." Her husband was forced to go with the bluecoats to search the swamp, and while he was gone the soldiers set fire to the gin house and its bales of cotton, and to the granary, with its bushels of wheat. Their slaves had begged for the bales of kersey cloth in the gin house before it was torched, contending the cloth was for their winter clothes. Unpersuaded, the bluecoats charged that it would be used to uniform the "Rebs." As Nora Canning looked on, a bummer sneered, "Well, madam, how do you like the looks of our little fire? We have seen a great many such, within the last few weeks."

"I told him I didn't care," she answered. "I was thankful that not a lock of that cotton would ever feed a Yankee factory or clothe a Yankee soldier's back."

Other plunderers roped the old judge's neck, threatening to tighten the knot further until he revealed the hiding place of his "gold." When he began to lose consciousness, a soldier warned, "We like to have carried that game too far" and released him. The housekeeper was threatened with death unless she showed where the family silver was hidden. Then the bummers cut all the well ropes and went off with the buckets. "There was no [other] water nearer than half a mile."

The next morning "a rough-looking man from Iowa came to the window and asked if he could be of any service to me. The Negroes were afraid to approach the house during the day, but came at night and brought us wood, and did all they could for me. I told the stranger we had no water and nothing to eat. He offered to bring some water if I would give him a bucket. I told him every vessel had been carried off, and we had nothing. He then left and in about an hour returned with a wooden pail, such as the Negroes use in carrying water to the fields. . . . I was thankful to get it and expressed my gratitude. . . ." The Iowan then took two envelopes from his pockets, one containing "parched coffee" and the other brown sugar. "I never appreciated a cup of coffee more than I did that one."

By the time the judge had finished his coffee, foragers were carrying away sacks of potatoes from the storehouse. The Iowan returned, offering, "If you give me a basket I will bring in some of those potatoes before they are all taken, for you will need them." Later he returned to forestall further depredations, a soldier from New York giving the Iowan his gun and advising him to use it. When Colonel Frederick C. Winkler of the 26th Wisconsin stopped by to inquire, Mrs. Canning told him she had nothing left to protect but their lives. He apologized for "Sherman's bummers," as he allegedly called them, and sent his men for coffee, sugar, rice, beef, flour, "and other articles." Winkler came again before his regiment broke camp "to see how we were getting on and said he had reported to Gen. Slocum . . . the indignities we had received and that the General was anxious to identify the parties. But, of course, that was impossible. . . ."

Other officers stopped by to "pay their respects," as they explained. One regretted the horrors that the war had brought to Southern families.

"You think the people of Georgia are faring badly," he said, "and they are, but God pity the people of South Carolina when this army gets there, for we have orders to lay everything in—not to leave a green thing in the State for man or beast. That State will be made to feel the fearful sin of Secession before our army gets through with it. Here our soldiers were held in check, as much as it is possible with such a large body of men, and when we get to South Carolina they will be turned loose. . . ." No such orders existed.

That Georgians in the wake of the march were faring badly was a common experience, although not often recalled as vividly—perhaps melodramatically—as by Nora Canning and Mary A. H. Gay, who published her memoir in 1894, thirty years after her despairing search for food on November 30, 1864. In Decatur, from which Sherman had jumped off, she found "nothing left in the city to eat. Yea, a crow flying over would have failed to discover a morsel with which to appease its hunger." Her Confederate bonds and bills were useless, but she had heard of a Rebel commissary in reoccupied Atlanta that would barter provisions for the wherewithal of war. Especially prized were minié balls (actually leaden cones) for muzzle-loading shotguns, expended by the hundreds of thousands before the city fell.

Accompanied by her young, nearly deaf-mute, "house servant" Telitha, each with large baskets in hand, and "two dull old case-knives," she plodded off toward Atlanta and "found . . . the very spot where the Confederate magazine stood, the blowing up which, by Confederate orders, shook the very earth." During the long walk, the cold and the sharp wind bit through their wraps, but Telitha discovered a hoard of expended miniés in an ice-covered marsh. Although their hands bled, the women dug until they filled their baskets almost too heavily to carry.

In relief and in pain, Miss Gay "cried like a baby, long and loud" as they tottered with their loads through the "desolated" city, inquiring as they went for directions to the commissary. There "a courteous gentleman in a faded grey uniform, evidently discharged because of wounds received in battle," asked what he could do for her.

"I have heard," she explained, "that you give provisions for lead, and I have brought some to exchange." By his long pause, Mary Gay understood that despite appearances, she and her slave girl were undergoing "a sympathetic scrutiny," and that she was recognized as a lady "to the manor born." When finally asked what she would like in exchange, she appealed timidly, "If you have sugar, and coffee, and meal, a little of each if you please. I left nothing to eat at home."

Her baskets of miniés were removed to be weighed, and returned filled to their brims with coffee, sugar, flour, meal, lard, "and the nicest meat I had seen in a long time."

"Oh, sir," Miss Gay exclaimed, "I did not expect so much." Handing her a certificate, he said, "You have not yet received what is due you." She could return for a similar bounty. "I lifted two of these baskets, and saw Telitha grasp the other one, and turned my face homeward."

HARASSING THE UNION REAR GUARD, small Confederate forces tracked Union movements and tried to limit the enemy from ranging far off route to forage and fire deeper into lower Georgia. Pickings were now meager, and as Federals pushed to the southeast they found little for their depleted supply wagons. Cypress swamps would replace fields of sweet potatoes and corn, and short rations might slow the bluecoats more than bullets. As far as the Ogeechee River, produce had been plentiful, but for dwindling fodder. Bridges over smaller streams were almost invariably burned to slow the columns down, yet Poe's efficient engineers laid down pontoon spans, interrupting the march on each occasion for only a few hours. Once the long supply trains and accompanying cattle had crossed, crews would disassemble the planks and pontoons, reload them on wagons, and continue on. Intact bridges would be wrecked after them to deter Wheeler's horsemen.

It seemed all but certain as the stretched-out columns approached Louisville in the direction of Millen, where Kilpatrick's raid had been thwarted, that their target was Savannah. In the period of the American Revolution, Millen, as it was later renamed, was described on maps as "Seventy-Nine"—its mileage from Savannah.

With the city, now the primary Confederate harbor after Charleston, the certain target, on November 28 its mayor, Richard D. Arnold, issued a proclamation to appear in local newspapers:

MARCHING ACROSS A PONTOON BRIDGE IN GEORGIA

Fellow-Citizens: The time has come when every male who can shoulder a musket can make himself useful in defending our hearths and homes. Our city is well fortified, and the old can fight in the trenches as well as the young; and a determined and brave force can, behind intrenchments, successfully repel the assaults of treble their number.

The general commanding this division has issued a call for men of every age, not absolutely incapacitated from disease, to report at once to Capt. C. W. Howard, at the Oglethorpe barracks, for the purpose of organizing into companies for home defence. I call upon every man not already enrolled in a local corps to come forward at once. . . . Organization is everything. Let us emulate the noble examples of our sister cities of Macon and Augusta, where the whole male population is in arms. By manning the fortifications we will leave the younger men to act in the field. . . .

No time is to be lost. The man who will not comprehend, and respond to the emergency of the times, is foresworn to his duty and to his country.

As Sherman's march proceeded, newspapers with Arnold's call to arms would be found in towns still with rail access to Savannah.

THE LEFT WING RUMBLED close to Louisville by the twenty-seventh, but eight bridges across the Ogeechee and its tributaries were found burned, delaying the columns. Some soldiers stepped gingerly over timbers that were still smoldering. As soon as the smaller streams were spanned at cost to nearby barns, bummers crossed to loot, alleging that townspeople rather than Rebels were responsible. Lack of local resistance suggested Rebel absence—but for a home on Broad Street torched for defiantly flying the Confederate flag. As the flames spread, officers ordered an empty warehouse demolished to contain the fire. Louisville was ransacked and ruined before pontooniers could get XIV and XX Corps into the town to restore order.

At Bostick, to the immediate south, Federals on November 29 found two sawmills and an estimated two million feet of cut lumber, and thousands of wooden pegs intended as fasteners. The conflagration was intense. At the village of Summertown, farther south, General Howard's XV Corps arrived the same day that a handful of Texans pulled out. It usually went hard with inhabitants if they had sheltered Confederate troops, and on a tip the Federals pursued the Rebels, capturing two. (Texans were despised by most Georgians as outlaws and not "true South." Renegade Texans had held the Georgia town of Rome hostage until paid a ransom.) Sue Sample of Newberry, South Carolina, had made the mistake of visiting the Georgia plantation of her sister-in-law just before the Federals came. "The beds were torn open, feathers all out. The bedsteads were chopped to pieces." There were no Rebs there. "They shot all the hogs in the pen. . . . We could hear nothing but guns all day, and the squeals of hogs." Miss Sample begged them not to take all their corn, and was promised "that they would not, as the wagons were all filled but one."

She was on the porch when Brigadier General John E. Smith of the Third Division, XV Corps, rode up with one of his aides and told her what she already knew: "Our men are carrying on a great destruction." He asked if she lived there. She explained that she was visiting from South Carolina. "He bowed, blushed, rode off. . . ." Smith's men, infantry from Illinois, Iowa, Ohio, Minnesota, Missouri, Indiana, and Wisconsin, were more vocal, telling her what they expected to do to South Carolina. "I would always have an answer ready, and had a quarrel with one. I do not think any race of people can swear as much as the yankees." Smith's division camped nearby that night, "and until 11 o'clock, the camp was ringing with music, which made our hearts bleed. A [Federal] guard was stationed around the house that night."

EXCEPT FOR THE FORMER SEVENTY-NINE, place names in Georgia were usually less informative than railway stations, known by numbers that diminished as the trackage reached a terminus. A flag stop between two more major depots might be identified as 9½. At a station near the Ogeechee, David Conyngham encountered the elderly John Wells, who had been a depot master when trains stopped there. His farm had been foraged bare, and he was watching his fence rails smolder. "They say you are retreating," he remarked, "but it is the strangest sort of retreat I ever saw. Why, dog bite them, the newspapers have been lying in this way all along. They allers fall back after the battle is over. It was that ar' idee that first opened my eyes. . . . Our army was always whipping the Feds, and we allers fell back."

Wells sneered at Confederate boasting as only humbug—"for here you are" and "hogs, potatoes, corn and fences all gone. I don't find any fault. I expected it all." He blamed Jeff Davis for "splitting the Union," contending that if South Carolina's secession had been ignored by the rest of the South, the state "would have been split in four pieces by this time." The "rich fellows making this war," he charged to Conyngham, were "keeping their precious bodies out of harm's way." Wells thought of going to Canada, his wife's home, but was "afraid of the ice and cold," and remained—"but I can tell you this country is getting too cussed hot for me. Look at my fence rails burning there." As for the Confederate torching of bridges in the path of the Federals, "there's that bridge you put across the river in less than two hours—they might as well try to stop the Ogeechee as you Yankees. The blasted rascals who burnt this yere bridge thought they did a big thing: a natural born fool cut in two had more sense in either end than any of them."

Wells would stay. "To bring back the good old times," he said, "it'll take the help of Divine Providence, a heap of rain, and a deal of elbow grease, to fix things up again."

AT TENNILE STATION (No. 10) on the Georgia Central, a black woman told Major Nichols that she saw Union prisoners abused, forced to remove their uniforms ("You've worn these long enough!") and exchange them for rags. When she was found giving them food, she was whipped, and she displayed the welts on her back. Another "old darkey" told Sherman, "Dem Yank some of 'em come down here and first burn the depot—den some more come and dey burn up *de well*—dem Yanks is de most *destructionest people* ever I see!"

"The fact is our men are reckless," Hitchcock acknowledged in his diary, "and every place we go is occupied by scouts and stragglers ahead of the advance guard. In this way the army has lost several hundred [as] prisoners, picked up by rebel cavalry." Sherman acknowledged casually, "Serves 'em right—hope they shoot 'em."

Hitchcock described the crisp weather on November 29 as "the perfection of campaigning." The pine barrens country had "good (sandy) roads, fine pure air, no difficult hills," and, he exaggerated, "[supply] trains well up, forage of every kind." They continued to bypass swamps, and bedded down on "pine straw" and soft "wire grass" that had only one "danger." Smokers, of whom there were very many, could spark a conflagration and the hasty upsetting of hundreds of tents. Alabama born, he found his first sighting of cypress swamps and Spanish moss as "old friends," evoking memories of his childhood on Mobile Bay.

* * *

ON THE LAST DAY of November, the 1st Alabama Cavalry, a Union force despite its name, reached the Ogeechee, where Rebels tried to fire a footbridge but succeeded only in charring both ends before withdrawing. As it would not support the mass of marchers nor the wagons or herds, the 1st Missouri Engineers under Orlando Poe laid a pontoon bridge just above it. With ten canvas "boats" and 195 feet of planking, it was ready in ninety minutes, to John Wells's admiration from the other side, at his brick railway depot—due for destruction the next day as the column moved on. Wells sat by Sherman's campfire after dark, full of jokes belying the ravaging of his property. "I told my wife," Wells observed, "these [Rebel] preachers said the God of battles was on our side and would be round playing the Devil, but you look for him tonight and he's out hid in the swamp." The general promised that Wells's cotton, all he had left, would be protected.

Railway stations were opportunities to retrieve abandoned Rebel

A SEEMINGLY ENDLESS COLUMN OF SOLDIERS
AND WAGONS MOVES EASTWARD

newspapers; Hitchcock found an Augusta paper only four days old. "Where is that fellow Sherman anyhow?" a column questioned. The Oconee, the writer urged, should become "Sherman's river of death." But Federal columns had now crossed both major rivers in lower Georgia preliminary to the last, the Savannah.

SIX

"... Just Like a Dose of Salts"

A UNION SOLDIER PUT INTO LIGHTHEARTED verse his feelings about the march, and his confidence in Sherman, attitudes that would have further embittered beleaguered Georgians in the path of the war:

> General Sherman is the man,
> He makes the Rebels waltz, sir!
> And leads his men through all the South,
> Just like a dose of salts, sir!

By the sixteenth day out, there seemed to be no effective opposition short of Savannah. Except for slaves who remained loyal to their masters (or who valued their food and shelter), and the immobile elderly, families alarmed by the approach of the Federals were without adult males at home. Still, pressing a "hard war" on the home front in the South as a tactic to bring it to a conclusion on the battle lines seemed to persuade few civilians and fewer soldiers. Collective casualties, North and South, were passing a million, but the Confederate military leadership had determined to fight on where it could, until no useful options existed or the Union soured on the cost. Lincoln's reelection closed off the hope of compromise. Sherman was also closing off a Rebel military option. Railways had helped make the conflict the first massive modern war, fought over long distances and with huge casualties inevitable, because troops and guns could be transported wholesale by locomotives and trackage. With its rail connections diminishing, the Confederacy was literally losing its steam.

Even across the Atlantic, where news arrived late and hope lingered among Southern sympathizers, the chief foreign organ for the Confederacy, *The Times* of London, was losing heart. "If this enterprise be brought to a successful termination," it editorialized with obvious reluctance, "*General Sherman will undoubtedly be entitled to the honour of having added a fresh chapter to the theory and practice of modern warfare.*" Nevertheless, it seized at a familiar straw. There was still a possibility that he would fail: "Instances, no doubt, have occurred where a bold general, under the pressure of some insuperable difficulty or the seduction of some irresistible temptation, has abandoned the base of his operations and undertaken a long and toilsome march in search of another base. . . . The attempt has generally been made in the hope of raising [rebellion in] a country disaffected to its existing government, and the prospect of almost entire security if the point sought for can once be reached." *The Times*, hopefully, it seemed, saw neither situation as likely. The Georgia population was entirely hostile, and at the other end of his march "he can count on no information or assistance of any kind." Yet the British, for whom the sea was essential to empire, and whose regime had long conspired, less than covertly, to supply the Confederacy in the face of suffocating Union blockade, could not help but know otherwise. A vast Federal supply fleet awaited Sherman in the Atlantic, the Southern coast now almost completely under Union control, and no one in the American command structure expected any more than resentful but helpless acquiescence in occupation.

On the eighteenth day out, December 3, troops reached Millen. Federals were appalled by the abandoned POW stockade. Soldiers examined the burrows that prisoners had crudely dug for shelter, and the graves of comrades who had died of hunger, exposure, and shooting (if they approached barrier "deadlines"). An officer wrote that one could not come away without a renewed "feeling of hardness" toward the Confederacy. The compound at Millen, Hitchcock wrote, proved "simply a *pen*, . . . high posts driven into the ground, close to each other, about 300 yards square; no shelter of any kind, no shed, nor tent, nor roof whatever. . . . There was no spring nor well nor any water inside the enclosure." He estimated 750 graves—"no head board nor other designation save that each fiftieth grave was so numbered." Photographer George N. Barnard, who had joined the columns from Atlanta, confessed, "I used to be very

DESTROYING THE RAIL DEPOT AT MILLEN JUNCTION

much troubled about the burning of houses, but after what I've seen, I shall not be much troubled by it."

Sherman had ordered Kilpatrick out again to feint toward Augusta, which worried some officers, not only because of his foolhardiness but because enemy skirmishers might be lying in wait. The cavalry moved north along Brier Creek and encountered Wheeler's men, who, outnumbered, resisted stubbornly, then moved their light artillery, suddenly in hazard, out of range. Federal losses, an officer acknowledged, were "quite heavy," while the Confederates left twenty-three dead and forty-one wounded on the field. Wheeler had been Kilpatrick's classmate at West Point, which gave the Union general an opening to send a courier through the lines under a flag of truce asking to attend a wounded officer who had been captured—"and at some future day you shall have the thanks of your old friend." The prisoner died, but his care left Wheeler the opportunity to declare—perhaps in implied contrast—that he had seen to it that his men fought with "principles of chivalry and true soldierly honor."

On the nineteenth day out, on a march for the right wing of sixteen miles, edging closer to the coast, troops reached the narrowing corridor between the Ogeechee and the Savannah rivers. The terrain of yellow pine, stiff wire grass, and sandy soil was giving way to swamps creeping across the banks of creeks that fed into rain-swollen rivers. It was Sunday, December 4. Federals were approaching Georgia Central station No. 5, which they would dismantle. The weather grew increasingly warm, and troops, no longer finding much to forage, and in little fear of Rebel marauders, built fires in late afternoon and began tenting—and even washing. "The streams are cool and clear by many a cliff and wood," the *New York World*'s correspondent wrote. "Here, 'naked and not ashamed,' a hundred soldiers bathe. . . . Their clothes and arms are flung along the banks; their bodies gleam and splash among the ripples. Their laughter rings harsh and loud, low and musical, while moving ranks upon the bridge above go by."

As campfires glowed in twilight, Hitchcock was mesmerized by the scene. "Drops of flame [were] scattered all over the large open fields they occupy, across which stand the dark, moving figures of men and horses. Presently up the road come shouting, laughing, singing—as if they were beginning a holiday—the troops who have been all day hard at work tearing up and destroying the railroads. They file off into their camps, and then the music of a fine band begins to swell upon the air, just far enough to lose all harshness. They are playing sacred airs—good old hymn tunes. . . ."

A melancholy, newly popular song redolent of the soldiers' time and place also had religious overtones. "We Shall Meet but We Shall Miss Him" recalled a symbolic "our noble Willie" in their evening prayers. As he and others had "upheld our country's honor," soldiers sang:

> Sleep today, oh early fallen,
> In thy green and narrow bed,
> Dirges from the pine and cypress
> Mingle with the tears we shed.

Hitchcock was "touched" by such sense of the divine. "If we go safely through this land, once of brothers, now of foes, it is of His mercy and not—Heaven knows—of our dessert." His chief liked music of all kinds. As a correspondent recalled, "Sitting before his tent in the glow of a camp fire one evening, General Sherman let his cigar go out to listen to an air that a distant band was playing. The musicians ceased at last. The general turned to one of his officers: 'Send an orderly to ask that band to play that tune again.'"

"The Blue Juniata" echoed "with exquisite variations." It had been the first popular song composed by an American woman. In 1844 Marion Dix Sullivan had imagined the river coursing through central Pennsylvania in early Colonial days, and at its banks an Indian maiden singing,

"Bold is my warrior. . . . Soft and low he speaks to me. . . ." Although it recalled a bygone era, the lyrics resonated to soldiers with loved ones back home. Soon the band repeated it, Hitchcock wrote, "even more beautifully than before. Again it ceased, and then, off to the right, nearly a quarter of a mile away, the voices of some soldiers took it up with words. The band, and still another band, played a low accompaniment. Camp after camp began singing; the music of 'The Blue Juniata' became, for a few minutes, the oratorio of half an army."

BRIGADIER GENERAL P. J. OSTERHAUS had taken his XV Corps (right wing) down the west bank of the Ogeechee to Statesboro, a hamlet of a few cabins and a small frame courthouse. A Union officer asked a resident for directions to Statesboro and was told, "You are standing in the middle of it." It was poor country. Major Connolly thought that the women and children "look utterly ignorant and stupid." Mounted foraging detachments were venturing deeper to find provisions, and on December 4 had to fight off an estimated six hundred Confederate horsemen. Eight foragers were wounded and twenty-seven others ridden down and captured. Among them was John Brooks, a black whom General Geary had hired in Georgia as a servant, and who was accompanying a captain from the 109th Pennsylvania. (In March 1865, Brooks, released, would turn up in New Cumberland, Pennsylvania, at Geary's home. The general was still with Sherman.)

At Wright's Bridge the next day, Federals found the span over the Ogeechee partly burned and again fought off Wheeler's cavalrymen, who fired from the edges of the march, then vanished into the pines. Bluecoats demolished several abandoned cabins for lumber and crossed the sluggish creek.

On December 5, they neared station 4½ on the Georgia Central. Advance scouts shouted in warning about a swamp ahead, "No bottom!"

The marshy terrain, Savannah's perimeter of natural defenses, had slowed down the columns. On the sixth there was little forward movement as they rested and reviewed their routes. On December 7, the twenty-second day of the march, as the pace picked up, General Davis prudently dismounted his foragers. The pickings were poor and, with skirmishers both from Wheeler's cavalry and from Savannah now harassing advance elements, Sherman approved. As they pressed on from creek to creek and improvised bridges over ferry landings, troops were trudging and tiring. A brigade of General Hazen's Second Division (Ohio, Indiana, and Illinois infantry) was deputed to clear obstructions from the roads, additionally boggy from pelting rain. As horses, cattle, wagons, and artillery began squishing into swampland, muddied troops had to push and pull rutted vehicles and mired mules.

Reaching the Georgia Central's stations 3 and 2, the Second Division was closing in on Savannah's outskirts, as was Brigadier General John M. Corse's Fourth Division (Iowa, Illinois, Indiana, and Ohio infantry).* When Federal cavalry approached a train with evacuees leaving the city for the South, and fired on it, the engineer stopped and reversed direction. Dismounting, Captain William Duncan led a mule onto the tracks, then shot it. Blocked, the locomotive and its eighteen carriages could not back toward Savannah, and the trapped passengers, including R. R. Cuyler, the railway's president, were taken prisoner. (Ironically, a steamer carrying his name had been outfitted in 1861 as a Union blockade gunboat.) The failed escape bore no resemblance to the cocky posture of the *Savannah News* a week earlier. "Sherman appears to be making no progress in his invasion of the State," the *News* had crowed in an effort to boost local morale. "He is no nearer the coast than he was several days

---

* Wounded at Allatoona, Georgia, on October 6, Corse had signaled Sherman after the shooting stopped, "I am short a cheekbone and an ear, but am able to whip all hell yet!"

ago. He appears to be hesitating and acting altogether as though he were caught in a bad box and don't know how to get out. Afraid to go forward and cannot go back, his men tired and hungry, with our forces rapidly closing in around him. All these things excite the liveliest hopes of his early destruction." A verse of "Marching through Georgia" would recall the Southern bravado:

> *"Sherman's dashing Yankee boys will never make the coast!"*
> *So the saucy rebels said, and 'twas a handsome boast*
> *Had they not forgot, alas! to reckon with the Host*
> *While we were marching through Georgia.*

East of station 2 on December 8, riding with Major General Francis Blair's XVII Corps, Sherman spent the night under the roof of the apparently friendly, but somewhat less than godly, Rev. Emanuel Heidt, a Methodist minister. Checking security, Sherman's aide, Lewis M. Dayton, found a cache of rifle cartridges hidden in the minister's chicken coop. Heidt was "badly scared," according to Hitchcock, and protested that he knew nothing about it. "Must have been done by your soldiers," he ventured.

"We don't draw ours from the Macon Arsenal," said Dayton, turning up the label on a packet of cartridges. "Better look into that, sir, it may compromise you," said Sherman. Heidt hurried off, then returned with the excuse that his absent son, John, had stored the ammunition there without his father's knowledge. Although Heidt's slaves confided that the minister was behind the torching of a bridge over a nearby creek, Heidt was a man of the cloth, and Blair did not order the house burned.

Thousands of self-liberated slaves—the "contrabands" who clung to the edges of the march—were obsessed with reaching Savannah. They slowed the slogging and reduced the available rations just as foraging became unrewarding, and Wheeler's horsemen, like the swarming of swamp

A TRAIN OF CONTRABANDS FOLLOW
THE REAR OF A FEDERAL COLUMN

insects, plagued the infantry and supply trains. The gunplay after dark, Major Connolly wrote, "was very annoying, as we were all very sleepy."

At midnight, as December 8 opened, troops of XIV Corps were roused, after two hours' sleep, on the order of General Davis. They were to march in silence to a pontoon-and-planks span at Ebenezer Creek, a tributary of the Savannah, thrown by Colonel George P. Buell's 47th Indiana. The approach across the marshland to the stream, deep enough almost to be a bayou, had been "corduroyed" with logs. Rain still fell but ended near dawn while troops and wagons still crossed in darkness. To Connolly it was "the most dismal cypress swamp I ever saw, on a narrow causeway, just wide enough for a wagon to drive along."

With Wheeler's cavalry reportedly once more in his rear, Davis hurried the awkward transit, determined to abandon his cumbersome appendage of black followers on the far side of the water. Sherman's Field Order No. 119, promulgated exactly a month earlier, specified, "All surplus servants, non-combatants, and refugees, should go to the rear, and none should be encouraged to encumber us on the march. At some future time we will be able to provide for the poor whites and blacks who seek to escape the bondage under which they are now suffering."

Riding forward, Connolly found the corps provost marshal, Major Lee, carrying out Davis's (and Sherman's) instructions to the letter by turning terrified blacks from the bridge. Connolly asked whether those huddled in the swamp could cross, and was told that Davis ordered that they be kept back—that the pontoons had to be taken up swiftly to thwart Wheeler. Realizing that disassembly "must result in all these negroes being recaptured or perhaps brutally shot down by the rebel cavalry," Connolly was appalled.

As morning came, about six hundred slaves, from the elderly and infirm to children, a relatively small number of the contrabands in the tailback of the corps, watched with increasing dread as fourteen thousand bluecoats and their horses, mules, cattle, artillery, and wagons finished rumbling over the hundred feet of the swaying span. When the last cow reached the eastern bank, Major Lee ordered the bridge cut loose and drawn to the eastern shore. Stranded, the blacks cried out helplessly, realizing that Rebel horsemen, few in numbers but surely armed and angry, were somewhere behind them. Someone in the crowd shouted in panic, "Rebel cavalry coming!"—and many, without knowing how to swim, and fully clothed, tried to ford swift-moving Ebenezer Creek. Some dismayed bluecoats on the eastern bank felled logs and pushed them across; a few blacks crossed on makeshift rafts of downed branches.

"Let the 'iron pen of history' write the comment on this action of a Union general," Connolly charged in his diary. Another officer wrote angrily that it was "a burning shame and a disgrace, and inhuman, to leave them to struggle in thirty feet of water for their lives; for they prefer sinking in the water to returning to slavery." A private from Minnesota condemned the order as "more completely inhuman and fiendish" than anything "in all the annals of plantation cruelty." Davis insisted afterward that he was only carrying out Sherman's judicious field order—and besides, he would soon need the pontoon equipment again. The swampy path to Savannah was crosscut by webs of marshes and streams.

When Wheeler's scouts reached the west bank of Ebenezer Creek, they found a hundred or more stranded blacks—mostly women, children, and elderly men—weeping and praying. The horsemen fired warning shots, then rode back to report. The remnant would be rounded up for return to their owners. XIV Corps slogged forward into the morning, some officers and men stewing angrily about Davis, whom Major Connolly called "an infernal copperhead." Ignoring the hazard to his career, Connolly wrote to his Illinois congressman, who supplied the text to the *New York Tribune*. Forwarded in full to the Senate Military Commission, the letter would turn the heat on Sherman.

In January, the general—who knew nothing of Ebenezer Creek—would receive a confidential message from Henry Halleck, whose dislike of Sherman was matched by Sherman's long-standing contempt for the timid chief of staff. After praising Sherman's "great march," Halleck reported that some officials in Washington were concerned that the general had "manifested an almost criminal dislike to the negro" in preventing fifty thousand slaves from accompanying troops to Savannah, withdrawing their labor from the South, while furnishing a work force, and potential soldiers, for the Union. Halleck referred in particular to Ebenezer Creek and General Davis's known prejudices. Outraged at Halleck's exaggerations, Sherman defended his subordinate and denied the charges. The numbers of camp followers were grossly inflated; the blacks would have impeded the march; Davis needed the pontoons for reuse.

Still, it was no secret that Sherman himself had always considered blacks an inferior race, unready for equal rights under the law.

However outmanned, and slowed by lack of bridges across Ebenezer Creek and other streams to the east, Wheeler's cavalry, which ranged at times from two hundred to two thousand horsemen, continued to harass the Federals, snatching unwary bluecoats on the edges of the columns, finally breaking off contact after a skirmish with the rear guard of XX Corps. He would not be back. Wheeler had been ordered by General Hardee to cross the Savannah River to the South Carolina side, protecting fragile approaches toward Savannah from the opposite bank, including King's Bridge, the major crossing. Below the river, by land from the west, there were five corridors to the city: two firmly based railway routes and three "dirt pikes"—narrow causeways across otherwise impassable swamps. All passages, Sherman knew, were protected close to Savannah by Hardee's formidable artillery.

ON THE MORNING of December 10, the twenty-fifth day out, Federals were nine miles from Savannah, approaching station 1 on the Georgia Central line. Governor Brown called on local jailers to release their prisoners, for conviction gave them a "permanent exemption from service," and the *Savannah Morning News*, echoing other Southern papers, proposed drafting slaves, rather than allow them to "increase and fatten as an idle spectator of the rapid exhaustion of power which rules over him," but rather than give them arms, the blacks should be assigned "the most servile and laborious duties" to relieve the "weak, overworked white men." Rather than save his best beverages for wassailing at Christmas, Mayor Richard Arnold, a Savannah physician educated in the North, sent the contents of his wine cellar upcountry to Augusta, writing the consignee, "The wines are above all price and I would dislike to have them sacrificed, independent of all pecuniary considerations."

Union troops were now encountering a treacherous new weapon concealed in the defensive obstacles of heaped tree trunks and branches obstructing the roads. Two "torpedoes"—primitive mines made in Augusta and concealed under the abatis—exploded, killing a horse and wounding several men in the 1st Alabama Cavalry (a Federal unit despite its name). Hearing what sounded like cannon shots, Hitchock and Sherman rode forward and found that an officer, Lieutenant Tupper, "*had his right foot torn off* just at or rather just above [his] ankle joint," and suffered two further shrapnel injuries. Enraged at what seemed a war crime, General Blair called for "greatly alarmed" Confederate prisoners to be brought forward, handed picks and shovels, and ordered to dig for more mines. "They begged hard," Sherman recalled, "but I reiterated the order," and they stepped "gingerly" as they worked. Without injury they extracted seven more. Hitchcock described "Southern chivalry" as nothing but an instinct for assassination. Sherman sent a prisoner into Savannah under a flag of truce to warn General Hardee how the Federals would be dealing with further torpedoes. The threat was ignored.

FLAGS OF TRUCE were still commonplace. From his camp overlooking Mobile Bay, Private Taylor wrote to his wife, "A Yankee flag of truce boat lay near here last night. She came to bring blankets and clothing for their men whom we have prisoners and to take potatoes to our men who are [Union prisoners] confined on Ship Island [in the Gulf of Mexico]. It looks curious to see men engaged in killing each other so to meet and be so friendly. This war is a shame, a disgrace to civilization. Oh! I wish to God it would end." He postscripted a further note: "I have some whiskers but not as many as usual. I wish you could get to nuzzle them."

Moving up from Alabama to look for his unit was Private Isaac Hermann, a small, thin, mustached German émigre who had become a Georgian. At a Confederate post he had encountered Major General

Abe Beaufort, a Kentuckian, who asked him, "Have you got a horse? We are cavalry." "No," Hermann said, "but I expect to get one the first fight we get into." Beaufort laughed at Hermann's feistiness and waved him on. As they moved in the direction of Andersonville, Hermann mused loyally that the Union was responsible for the "unfortunate" conditions at Confederate prison camps, having ceased to exchange most prisoners because freed Rebels would augment the replacement-starved South.

With a horse he somehow acquired, Hermann cantered ahead in the darkness and came upon "about half a regiment of cavalry," tethered his mount, and stretched out on an empty blanket by a fire. "Hello, comrade, you are lying on my blanket," said a Federal soldier. Concealing his surprise, Hermann stretched out his arms as if awakening and said evasively to the men nearby, who were used to German accents, "This is a terrible life to lead. Where are we going?" He heard someone say, "Savannah. . . . Did you not get three days' rations? We are going to advance."

Cautiously, in the flickering firelight, Hermann remarked, "I'm afraid some of us will never get there. I heard that there is an army of fifteen thousand rebels ahead of us within fifteen miles." While lying extravagantly about the numbers, he was hoping to encounter some Southerners again. "That would not amount to much with what we have," said the soldier. As soon as Hermann could, he slipped away, remounted his horse, offered a cock-and-bull story to two sentinels, and rode off to warn Beaufort's troops.

THE UNION IN ITS VASTNESS held Confederate prisoners of war from the top to the bottom of its domains. President Lincoln on December 6 was visited by Noah Brooks, a reporter for the Sacramento, California, *Daily Union* who had regular entreé to the White House. "Here is one speech of mine which has never been printed," Lincoln said, handing him a pencil jotting. "On Thursday of last week two ladies from Tennessee came before the President asking the release of their officer husbands held as prisoners of war at Johnson's Island. [The stockade in Sandusky Bay, Lake Erie, held three thousand captives on half the island's 300 acres.] They were put off until Friday, when they came again; and were put off until Saturday. At each of the interviews one of the ladies urged that her husband was a religious man. On Saturday the President ordered the release of the prisoners, and then said to this lady, 'You say your husband is a religious man; tell him when you meet him, that I say I am not much of a judge of religion, but that, in my opinion, the religion that sets men to rebel and fight against their government, because, as they think, that government does not sufficiently help *some* men to eat their bread on the sweat of *other* men's faces, is not the sort of religion upon which people can get to heaven.'"

AT HER FARMSTEAD in southern Georgia, Laura Buttolph felt little less in harm's way than her aunt, Mary Jones, a Presbyterian minister's widow who resided at one of her three plantations in Liberty County, about thirty miles south of Savannah. On December 10, Laura was offered the discouraging advice from a Rebel captain "that the Yankee officers would station guards around the private residences while the army passed[,] if requested." It sounded ominous, she wrote. "If it is God's will, I hope we may fall in with the best of them." As Mrs. Jones's son Charles, Jr., now a lieutenant colonel, was artillery commander at Savannah, Laura hoped that the Yankees "get whipped at Savannah. May God shield my beloved cousin from death, and take care of us and all our loved ones!" Provisions had been grossly wasted by both sides, she deplored, and "starvation staring us in the face, is what I dread. Many have gone to Thomasville [the nearest town]; but the crowd is so great there, and board a hundred dollars a day, we might as well die of want in one place as other."

Mrs. Jones's daughter, Mary Mallard, wife of an Atlanta clergyman, had fled from the city to one of her family's plantations. On December 15, "a stalwart Kentucky Irishman"—obviously a bummer—intruded to demand, "Have you any whiskey in the house?" Although she insisted she had none, he intended to search, and demanded the keys to every cupboard and trunk, even to her sewing machine. While he ransacked, another "Yankee" joined him, "a young Tennesseean," then "five Yankees dressed as Marines," possibly "rigged . . . from some house before coming here." All asked for food, and took what was being prepared for dinner.

One intruder discovered a "secession rosette" that Mrs. Mallard's brother, Charles, had worn when mayor, and pinned it on his uniform. It gave them occasion to argue with Mrs. Jones about secession, which she claimed as the right of sovereign states, and she would not be goaded into denying the morality of slavery. It was, for her, after all, condoned in the higher law of the Bible. Finding nothing further they wanted indoors, the bummers claimed the horses in the field. When all seemed too old to be useful, they took an aged mule instead, abandoning it at the gate.

Weeks earlier in the march General Howard had issued his Order No. 26: "Having come to the knowledge of the major general commanding that the crimes of arson and robbery have become frequent throughout this army, it is hereby ordered that hereafter any officer or man of this command discovered in pillaging a house or burning a building without proper authority, will, upon sufficient proof thereof, be shot." Although he had it read to all troops, apparently no proof sufficient for charges ever emerged.

The next day a detachment of Union cavalry came—Kilpatrick's unruly men, "flying hither and thither, ripping open the safe with their swords and breaking into the crockery cupboards. Fearing we might not have a chance to cook," Mrs. Mallard wrote in her diary, "Mother had some chicken and ducks roasted and put in the safe for our family." However absurd, it was too obvious a hiding place. "All yelling, cursing, quarreling," the cavalrymen tore the "secesh" birds apart with their teeth, and then clamored for whiskey. Finding none in the abstemious household, they broke open "everything that was closed," now searching for jewelry. Terrified, the women appealed for a cavalry officer to intervene, but the looters "said they were all officers and would do as they pleased." Finally they carried off their plunder, mostly men's clothes, after one of the party made "a little show of authority, which was indicated by a whip which he carried." Similar reminiscences of Northern outlawry fill Southern diaries, memoirs, and letters. Even if details were colorfully embellished in the retelling, the uncivil war was being brought violently and uselessly home.

The Federals were now edging closer to Savannah. Its prewar population of thirty thousand, a quarter of them slaves, had been depleted, but its outlying farms and plantations had swelled with refugees from occupied or threatened regions elsewhere in Georgia. Although running low on precious candles, Mrs. Jones had written to her sister-in-law, Susan Cummings, "God's dealings with me and mine are very solemn. . . . Charles stands before a murderous foe, every moment exposed to death if called into battle; of this there can scarcely be a doubt, for their cannon are already firing at intervals."

Desperate for reinforcements to defend Savannah River crossings, the Confederate command in South Carolina had recruited and was training a battalion of 1,100 foreign volunteers who, Mary Chesnut acknowledged from Columbia, had "a capital band of music" but were otherwise "a mistake." She took no comfort in their presence. Although the *Richmond Despatch* of December 12 reported Union troops as twelve miles from Savannah and protecting Sherman's rear from "the remorseless ravages of Wheeler who has hunted and hung on him like a bloodhound," it was still unclear as to whether he would attack or bypass the city. To Mrs. Chesnut the foreign fighters "don't ever give Sherman a thought" and

FEDERALS PLODDING THROUGH THE SWAMPS

seemed more interested in romancing Southern ladies than in drilling. "We met a squad of the Foreign Legion going to guard the Prestons' house. Is it not putting a cat to take care of the cream?" (The Prestons had attractive, teenage daughters.) The dismal news from Tennessee and Georgia could not be concealed by any of the newspapers Mrs. Chesnut saw, which claimed small successes and forecast inevitable enemy frustrations and defeats. "The deep waters are closing over us," she wrote, unpersuaded.

The Rebel press had predicted almost daily that Sherman's march into the unknown would run out of provisions. There were too many men and animals to feed, and little forage in marshes and savannahs. Despite having laid in a long supply train, Union troops and their wagon teams were beginning to get hungry. Fodder for horses, mules, and cattle was now low, as swampland furnished little but rice, and General Hardee in Savannah had even ordered levees and sluices opened and rice fields flooded to inundate roads and impede foraging. At high tide, with the Atlantic near, even normal inundations could exceed six feet. Union general Carlin described rice as "more aquatic than agricultural."

While camped near a swamp where Rebel cavalry had occupied abandoned slave quarters, Iowans found that horses had been quartered in a soggy field in which "nigger beans" (cowpeas) had been raised. Some of the unpicked "blackeyed" harvest could be seen in the weeds and manure. Troops dug them out eagerly. According to Sergeant Bull, issued only three hardtacks daily, "Cowpeas would never be eaten by a human being unless he was in a starving condition." His New Yorkers boiled the leavings into a thick yellow porridge that resembled mud, spooning it down "with satisfaction."

In his memoirs, Sherman dismissed some of the realities about rations and terrain. "As we approached Savannah," he wrote, "the country became more marshy and difficult, and more obstructions were met in the way of felled trees, where the roads crossed the creeks, swamps, or narrow causeways, but our pioneer companies were well organized, and removed these obstacles in an incredibly short time. No opposition from the enemy worth speaking of was encountered until the heads of columns were within fifteen miles of Savannah, where all the roads leading into the city were obstructed more or less by felled timber, with earth-works and artillery. But these were easily turned and the enemy driven away."

There were, indeed, few casualties, and few of the enemy encountered short of Savannah, but Sherman had no access to service diaries like that of Private Frederick Buerstatte, who wrote, "Our rations are now short and one discovers what hunger feels like. . . . We now have too little to live on and too many dying. We have only a small amount of rice and an ounce of meat per day." (The dead and dying were insubstantial rumor, which spread easily as troops grew hungry.) John Peters complained,

"Our rations run out and we have none to draw. We have rice instead of hard tack." To crave the saltless flour-and-water biscuit that was the ration staple of last resort, softened in coffee or water, was evidence of Northern aversion to rice. No one died of malnutrition, but talk among troops about shortages seemed less imaginary as their diet dwindled and dry wood for cooking and campfires became scarce.

Soldiers now had to learn how to use the soggy rice, hulling it in hollowed-out logs with rifle butts, then piling the residue on blankets that were beaten to separate the kernels from the chaff. Even tasteless hardtack often discarded earlier, or offered to horses, now seemed preferable to what one bluecoat deplored as "boiled rice for dinner, boiled rice for supper, . . . rice on toast without the toast, for breakfast, for dinner, rice, for supper, rice." Otherwise they had beef on the hoof to slaughter and serve. Neither rice nor coffee, cooked in sluggish swamp water, lost their unwelcome traces of cypress no matter how long they were boiled.

Preparing meals consumed much of a squad's time in the boggy outskirts of Savannah, and bluecoats now regretted their thoughtless waste on the march. Having planned his timing closely, Sherman was counting upon the supply ships of Rear Admiral John A. Dahlgren, due to arrive offshore well before Christmas and await signals from land forces to make contact. Some troops could now hear, or claimed they could hear, the roar and withdrawal of the sea.

Major Nichols reported in his diary on December 10 that the two wings had connected their lines and were beginning to probe Savannah's defenses:

> The necessity of open communication with the fleet is becoming apparent, for the army is rapidly consuming its supplies, and replenishment is vitally important. Away in the distance, across the rice fields as far as the [outer] banks of the Ogeechee, our signal-officers are stationed, scanning the

seaward horizon in search of indications of the presence of the fleet, but thus far unsuccessfully. On the other side of the river, within cannon range, stand the frowning parapets of Fort McAllister, its ponderous guns and rebel garrison guarding the only avenue open to our approach.

This evening a movement of the greatest importance has begun. Hazen's division of XV Corps is marching to the other side of the river. Fort McAllister must be taken. Tomorrow's sun will see the veterans whom Sherman led upon the heights of Missionary Ridge* within striking distance of [the fort's] walls. Warm words have been uttered by the Generals of XV and XVII Corps because the second division has been assigned the honor of this expedition. The possibility of repulse, the fear of wounds and death, do not seem to be considered. . . .

The night before, reaching the Savannah where it ran nearly parallel to the Ogeechee, General Howard had drawn up a brief dispatch to Dahlgren: "We have met with perfect success thus far. Troops in fine spirits and near by." (He thought later that he had logically put "Sherman" before "near by," but his copy hastily omitted his chief's name.) To get the message to Dahlgren, Howard needed a resolute few to make their way to the Atlantic and locate a Federal vessel. The "needle in the haystack" cliché applied. He chose Captain William Duncan, who had taken the surrender at Milledgeville, Sergeant Myron J. Amick, and Private George W. Quimby. A "long dugout, rather narrow and somewhat weather-beaten," plucked from an inlet, furnished the means.

Beginning in darkness, they were to drift as silently as possible down

* In Tennessee in November 1863.

the Ogeechee past Confederate security points, "torpedo" obstructions, the King's Bridge (already partly demolished by Confederate sappers), and Fort McAllister, into Ossabaw Sound and then into the sea. "It seemed next to impossible," Howard recalled, ". . . but Captain Duncan's already distinguished career as a scout and his confidence that he could accomplish the enterprise led me to try him."

WITH AN ADDITIONAL MESSAGE to Dahlgren from a signals officer, the three set out. On the morning of the tenth they came ashore near Fort McAllister, and unable to slip by, found some apparently free blacks (a thousand lived in the Savannah area) who offered to guide them. They flattened themselves behind bushes as a Hardee patrol passed; then—Howard recalled—the Federals were led "to quite a sizable negro house, went in, and were well treated and refreshed with provisions . . . [until] startled by hearing a party of Confederate cavalry riding toward the house. Of course they expected to be instantly captured, but the negroes coming quickly to their rescue concealed them under the floor." The Rebel cavalrymen stopped, found nothing suspicious, and continued on. Despite the risk, the friendly blacks guided Howard's men back to their boat.

As Duncan's crew continued on, hoping to locate the fleet, the siege of Savannah was beginning.

SEVEN

Besieging Savannah

URVIVING HAIRBREADTH ESCAPES, CAPTAIN Duncan's party hid during daylight on the eleventh, and in darkness paddled across the widening Ogeechee, narrowly evading oarsmen from a Confederate gunboat at anchor below Fort McAllister. Soon after dawn they drifted into the broad Ossabaw Sound, encountering the *Dandelion*, one of Admiral Dahlgren's dispatch boats cruising in search of some sign of Sherman. Hoisted aboard, the three were ferried to the flagship *Philadelphia*, in harbor at Port Royal, above Hilton Head, beyond the South Carolina border. Attempting to blockade Charleston, fifty miles to the north, in one of the earliest amphibious operations of the war, a fleet of seventy-four vessels under Rear Admiral Samuel F. du Pont with twelve thousand bluecoats aboard, had seized the harbor at Beaufort, "Port Royal," in November 1861.

Weighing anchor, Dahlgren's fleet prepared to sail toward Savannah, its signal rockets readied to alert Sherman's for-

ward units. In the opposite direction, the admiral sent a packet boat
north to the closest Union telegraph facility on the Virginia coast. On
December 12 the Executive Mansion received the long-awaited wire:

> I have the great satisfaction of conveying to you informa-
> tion of the arrival of General Sherman near Savannah, with
> his army in fine spirits. . . . This memorable event must be
> attended by still more memorable consequences, and I con-
> gratulate you most heartily on its occurrence.

Brigadier General John Gray Foster added a message from Hilton
Head to Henry Halleck, that Captain Duncan, of "Howard's scouts," reported that Sherman was ten miles from Savannah, and "advancing to
attack it." By the fourteenth, Duncan's feat made most Northern newspapers.

GENERAL BEAUREGARD had arrived in Savannah from South Carolina
on December 9, pondering anxiously William Hardee's few options for
the city. Hardee had left only one access route unflooded, counting upon
the cannon at Fort McAllister to keep Sherman's troops, some now six
miles distant, from replenishment by sea. Since trenches, rifle pits, artillery, and log barriers would only slow the overwhelming Federals, Hardee
planned to evacuate his men across to South Carolina by whatever shipping he could assemble. As he had, at best, 10,000 effective troops (Sherman's estimate was 18,000), many—but for seasoned artillerymen—only
poorly trained recruits, Beauregard urged Hardee to avoid entrapment
by improvising a multistaged pontoon bridge across the Savannah River.
For evacuation by water there were not enough boats available for many
miles, and the ferrying process would be hazardously slow. The Federals were close enough that Captain John Fox of the 2nd Massachusetts

would write home in a letter that he could not yet mail, "All right so far. . . . I am well though rough and dirty. No casualties in the 'Old Second.' We can hear the bells ring in the city."

Hearing things from afar very differently, unemployed General Lovell reported on the twelfth to Mary Chesnut's circle in South Carolina that Hardee had asked Jefferson Davis for his services, and, "in such a sanguine mood," as Lovell was expecting a return to action, reported "such good news. . . . He said Savannah was safe—we have men enough there." Besides, "Dick Taylor was behind Sherman with another army."

Taylor had arrived at Savannah almost alone, and had quickly departed. Hardee's army was pathetically small, and the abortive Confederate messiah who had been briefly at Macon was not pursuing Sherman with "another army." Recognizing wishful thinking, Mrs. Chesnut's lively young Charleston friend Isabella Martin scoffed about the Taylor rumor, "Where did he get it? How these people manufacture men in buckram!"

No such optimism was in evidence in Richmond. Since the loss of Savannah had seemed inevitable to Secretary of the Navy Stephen R. Mallory, he telegraphed grimly to the commander of local naval forces, "Should the enemy get and hold Savannah, and you can do no further service there, you are expected to dispose of your squadron to the greatest injury to him and to the greatest benefit to our country. If necessary to leave Savannah, your vessels, except the *Georgia*, may fight their way to Charleston. Under no circumstances should they be destroyed until every proper effort to save them shall have been exhausted." The orders were clear: at the very least, the ironclad floating battery *Georgia*, with little mobility and unlikely to make it into the Atlantic and to a safe harbor, was to be scuttled. Realistically, there were now no Southern safe harbors.

Fort McAllister's guns blocked Union passage from the Atlantic into Savannah. Although General Hazen had been assigned the coveted operation to overwhelm it, the chance for glory dazzled General Kilpatrick, who offered to seize the fort with his horsemen, if backed by a battalion of General Howard's infantry. A deserter had reported that little more than 200 men defended the fort, although backed by big guns. Kilpatrick proposed his operation to Sherman on the eleventh, claiming Howard's approval, but Howard, uninterested in being "Lil' Kil's" partner, went personally to Sherman to support Hazen.

To reach the fort, King's Bridge across the Ogeechee, only partly wrecked, had to be repaired. Howard ordered work begun. On December 12, Hazen was directed "to proceed against Fort McAllister and take it." Troops of the 58th Indiana under the direction of Captain C. B. Reese of the First Missouri Engineers felled hundreds of trees to improvise a new span and dismantled nearby houses for planks to repair the thousand board feet of the shattered bridge. On the morning of December 13, five companies of Hazen's troops from his Second Division crossed the jury-rigged span. To evade shelling, Sherman and Howard, with Brigadier General Giles A. Smith,[*] several staff officers, and Theodore R. Davis, war artist for *Harper's Weekly*, cantered via a circuitous twenty-mile route to the Langdon Cheves rice mill on the north bank of the Ogeechee. There, from the roof, they could watch, with field glasses, the assault on the opposite side.

Since the fort's twenty-three fixed barbette guns, pointed downriver toward Ossabaw Sound, were useless to defend against a land attack, formidable mortars covered the ground approaches. Pinewoods nearby had been leveled for a field of fire. For a siege, the defenders had forty-seven days' rations on hand, and forty gallons of whiskey. At about noon, Rebel response to the first sight of the oncoming Federals began. Union artillery from three miles off fired volleys as a diversion and to attract the attention of the Union fleet offshore.

---

* Smith was commander of the 1st Brigade, Second Division.

As the afternoon sun began to sink behind the distant woods, and infantrymen positioned themselves to storm the fort, both Sherman and Hazen from their vantages opposite saw "a movable smoke, like that from a steamer," closing in from the mouth of the Ogeechee. When the vessel came close enough to draw Confederate fire, the red flag of a navy signalman waved from its deck. Signal officers onshore recognized the small boat as from Dahlgren's fleet. It was the tender *Flag* from the *Dandelion*, with General Foster aboard. Earlier, it had intercepted Duncan's party and taken them aboard. Signal Corps lieutenant George Fisher, on deck, inquired visually, "Who are you?" Via the optical telegraphy, questions and answers traveled back and forth in minutes.

From the roof of the mill a signalman wagged, "Lieutenant [J. M.] McClintock, General Howard's signal officer. How can I get to you?" Fisher signaled—and then "What troops are at Fort McAllister?" McClintock responded, "We are now investing Fort McAllister with Hazen's division." Foster ordered the overly ambitious signal, "We are ready to render you any assistance." Sherman ordered back, "Can you assist us with your heavy guns?" McClintock answered for Foster, "Being a tugboat, no heavy guns aboard." From the tender, Foster's flagman waved, "Is Fort McAllister taken yet?" Sherman directed his signalman to whip his flags, "No, but it will be in a minute."

Hazen gave orders for frontal attack. Troops broke through the obstructing ditches and abatis, several infantrymen being killed instantly when their boots struck buried "torpedoes." Most bluecoats scurried safely inside, and in less than half an hour they were seen on the parapets yelling and firing into the air—a "*feu de joie*," as Major George Nichols put it. The joy was soon amplified by the gallons of whiskey in the captured booty. A soldier shouted as nine regimental flags were raised, "Take a big drink, a long breath, and then yell like the devil!" Yet the quick success, despite the daunting numbers, did not come easily. The defenders fought hand-to-hand until overpowered. Official accounts softened the

ASSAULT ON FORT MCALLISTER BY HAZEN'S TROOPS

statistics,[*] but according to General Howard 24 Union officers and men died in the assault, and 110 were wounded. Confederate casualties were 17 killed, 110 wounded, and 197 taken prisoner.

SHERMAN ORDERED A SKIFF to row him to the fort to see for himself. Then he met the tender at a landing, and hastily wrote several dispatches to local commanders and to General Grant and General Halleck in Washington for transmittal via the fleet. "Were it not for the swamps," he contended to Halleck, dating his message 11:50 PM on December 13, "we could march into the city; but as it is I would have to assault at one or two places, over narrow causeways, leading to much loss; whereas in a

---

* And other accounts invented dialogue and flag signal variations.

day or two with my communications restored, and the Batteries in position within short Range of the city, I will demand its surrender." He then fudged the facts somewhat. "The army is in splendid order, and equal to any thing. Weather has been fine and supplies abundant. Our march was most agreeable, and we were not at all molested by Guerillas. . . . We have on hand plenty of meat, salt and potatoes. All we need is bread and I have sent to Port Royal for that. We have not lost a wagon on the trip but have gathered in a large supply of negros, mules, horses, &c and our teams are in far better condition than when we started. My first duty will be to clear the army of surplus negros, mules and horses. . . , I hope by Christmas to be in possession of Savannah, and by the New Year to be ready to resume our Journey. . . ."

After dark at Hazen's farmhouse quarters, Sherman found Major George W. Anderson, the captured commander of the McAllister garrison, and praised the gallantry of his men. Howard recalled that he and Sherman "encamped in a rough way [with Hazen] after the soldier's fashion for the night." Rolled into a blanket, Sherman was hardly asleep when he was awakened by a messenger. General Foster, whose troops were aboard the fleet's outlying transports, had sailed within safe distance and begged Sherman to join him. Foster was too lame from an old Mexican War wound to come ashore easily.

Sherman sprang up, left Howard to work on the siege of Savannah, and was ferried by the *Dandelion* into the sound, where Foster was waiting on the *W. W. Nemaha*. Army quartermasters, Sherman learned, had shipped to Hilton Head, to refit his troops, 30,000 uniforms, 100,000 pairs of shoes and socks, 60,000 shirts and undershorts, 20,000 caps, 10,000 overcoats, 20,000 blankets, 10,000 tents, and other clothing and equipment. The cargo was a beginning—not nearly enough for all of the Federals, but after two months or more utterly necessary. As they steamed out to confer with Dahlgren, a shipment of clothing and rations to the Ogeechee docks was quickly arranged with Foster. Yet Sherman's impulsive departure came with a price. He had lost control of the impending Savannah assault.

At noon they reached the admiral's flagship, *Harvest Moon*, where, as Sherman wrote to his wife, he was received by officers and crew who "manned the yards & cheered, the highest honors at sea." To force a surrender, he asked for a shipment of guns heavier than could have been hauled overland from Atlanta, for as he wrote to Ellen, "The strength of Savannah lies in its swamps which can only be crossed by narrow causeways all of which are swept by heavy artillery. I came near being hit the 1st day, in approaching [Savannah] too near to reconnoiteer. A negro[']s head was shot off close by me." He wanted to disable the enemy guns.

In the admiral's quarters, Sherman was exultant at his reception, predicting that after Savannah, his course through the Carolinas to connect with Grant's divisions in Virginia would pinch off the rest of the Confederacy. All Rebels in his path would regret that they had started the war. "The whole army," he wired Halleck, "is crazy to be turned loose in Carolina; and with the experience of the past 30 days, I judge that a month's sojourn in South Carolina would make her [citizens] less bellicose. The Editors in Georgia profess to be indignant at the horrible barbarities of Sherman's army, but I know the people don't want our visit repeated."

ALTHOUGH NEWS—AND RUMORS—spread quickly among the bluecoats, some encamped on whatever dry land could be found about Savannah did not yet know about the capture of Fort McAllister. John Peters, with the 10th Illinois four miles from the city, thought that all was "quiet along the banks. Some of our boys go down to the coast and get some fresh Oysters . . . and fix a camp fire." (Oyster Bed Island was nearby in the Savannah.) Most soldiers had never seen an oyster or knew how to prepare the exotic objects. On December 15, Peters reported hearing artillery fire, and receiving "a few sweet potatoes"—but "the horses and mules have had nothing to eat for three days." Soon the draft animals and the cattle would be fed rice straw.

On Sherman's return he found that an initial shipload of rations, and mail held for his troops in Nashville, had been landed by the steamer *Fulton*. The mail, 278 postal sacks weighing fifteen tons, had been diverted to New York after rail lines from Tennessee southward had been severed. Troops zealously plunged into reading their letters and writing responses impossible for more than a month. "It was the oddest feeling in the world," Major Hitchcock wrote to his wife, "to see New York papers again—one felt as if he had been buried alive and resurrected. I had a real fellow feeling for Rip Van Winkle." An issue of the *New York Herald* had a map of "Sherman's Triumphant March," which Hitchcock was pleased

GENERAL FOSTER GREETS SHERMAN ABOARD THE *NEMAHA*
AFTER THE CAPTURE OF FORT MCALLISTER

to see, as press speculation had been so helpfully inaccurate. "It was a frantic sight, men snatching letters, whooping at the first touch with home," Major Tom Osborn wrote to his clerical brothers in St. Louis, happy to communicate again "with the known world." An Illinois soldier recalled the "curious spectacle" of "half-starved boys . . . reading their letters held in one hand while devouring hard-tack from the other."

Colonel Absalom H. Markland, overseeing the mail shipment, introduced himself to Sherman. "I've brought you a message from the President," he began. "He asked me to take you by the hand wherever I met you and say, 'God bless you and the army.' He has been praying for you."

"I thank the President," said the general. "Say my army is all right." To his further surprise, Sherman received a message from Grant dated December 3, and another dated three days later, urging him to bypass Savannah and let the city wither. He was to move north by sea, to "close out" General Lee in Virginia, leaving only a fortified base in Georgia or on the Carolina coast to harass the Rebel interior. "With the balance of your forces come here by water with all dispatch. . . . I want you in person." The ripe plum of Savannah dangled before Sherman, but Grant, stymied at Petersburg, seemed unable to dislodge Lee and take Richmond, the key—for him—to concluding the war. While reading Grant's unwelcome proposal, Sherman shouted at his aide, Lewis Dayton, "Won't do it, goddam it! I'll not do anything of the kind."

Happily for Sherman, Grant had left a loophole: "Unless you see objections to this plan which I cannot see, use every [supply] vessel going to you for purposes of transportation."

"The contents of these letters," Sherman recalled discreetly, for President Grant was ensconced in the White House as the memoir went to the publisher, "gave me great uneasiness, for I had set my heart on the capture of Savannah . . . ; for me to embark for Virginia by sea was so complete a change from what I had supposed to be the course of events that I was very much concerned." He began to implement Grant's proposal superficially while effectively undoing it. On December 16, as his troops were unloading fresh rations and reading withheld but newly delivered mail, he wrote to Grant, counting upon the slow communications by sea via Virginia, "I have initiated measures looking principally to coming to you with fifty or sixty thousand infantry, and incidentally to capture Savannah if time will allow."

Time indeed would allow, as Sherman claimed that he would need at least one hundred ships, their collection and dispatch surely taking many weeks. He confessed "a personal dislike to turning northward," but would keep Grant's deputy, Lieutenant William Dunn, nearby to carry further messages "until I know the result of my demand for the surrender of Savannah, but, whether successful or not, [I] shall not delay my execution of your order of the 6th, which will depend alone upon the time it will require to obtain transportation by sea."

Unaware of the contrary pressure from Grant, the Northern press predicted that Sherman would push into the Carolinas. Once the dispatch steamer *Eliza Hancock* arrived in Virginia from Dahlgren's fleet with news of the capture of Fort McAllister, a correspondent at Fortress Monroe reported on the seventeenth, "No doubt is entertained at Hilton Head but that Savannah must speedily fall, and when that takes place the attention of Sherman will in all probability be turned toward Charleston."

Although General Halleck had little influence with Grant, Sherman wrote to ask for his intervention to continue the operation into the Carolinas. "I attach much more importance [than does Grant] to these deep incisions into the enemy's country, because this war differs from European wars in this particular. We are not fighting armies, but a hostile people, and must make old and young, rich and poor, feel the hard hand of war. . . ." Sherman told Grant that he would seek the surrender of Savannah without further fighting, assuming that Hardee would concede that the fall of Fort McAllister had doomed the city. Yet, with far fewer, and less experienced, troops, Hardee showed no signs of wavering. For defense, the waterlogged countryside itself seemed worth a corps.

Savannah lay between the Ogeechee River to the south and the Savannah River to the north, opposite the Carolina shore. Mist rose from the marshland day and night, making literal the proverbial fog of war. Dense stands of pine shielded most Federals, fortunately, for at high tide the sidewheeler gunboats *Savannah* and *Sampson* steamed upriver to fire at troops of the left wing, which had to dig into the mud for protection. Bombardment from land sites suggesting in its intensity more artillerymen than Hardee actually had kept the right wing on edge. Intermittent cold rain further complicated visibility. Each side fired at flashes, or toward the sources of the crack or boom of weapons. "Please excuse this note," General Geary wrote to his wife, Mary, on December 16. "I write it on my knee sitting on a log with *only* 12 of the enemy's cannon firing over my head. You would think all pandemonium was loose if you were here."

Rebel artillery had greater range and explosive power than the lighter guns trundled from Atlanta, as Private Upson also found when an officer warned his unit at night to keep heads down. "He was going to wake up the Johnnys. He fired both of his guns at a Battery perhaps half a mile away. He woke them up all right. They replied, knocked the muzzle off the gun next to us, the wheel off the other, blew up the caisson standing in the rear of the guns, and threw one shell into the muck in front of us which exploded and covered us with about 20 tons of black mud. We were not hurt but are quite sure the Johnnys were not asleep at all."

On December 17, sending an aide under a flag of truce after withdrawing orders for direct assaults, Sherman confidently and somewhat untruthfully forwarded an ultimatum to Hardee:

> General, You have doubtless observed . . . that sea-going vessels now come through Ossabaw Sound and up the Ogeechee

to the rear of my army, giving me abundant supplies of all kinds, and more especially heavy ordnance necessary for the reduction of Savannah, I have already received guns that can cast heavy and destructive shot as far as the heart of your city; also I have for some days held and controlled every avenue by which the people and garrison of Savannah can be supplied, and I am therefore justified in demanding the surrender of the city of Savannah, and its dependent forts; and shall wait a reasonable time for your answer, before opening with heavy ordnance. Should you entertain the proposition, I am prepared to grant liberal terms to the inhabitants and gar-

SLOCUM'S ARMY CROSSING THE SAVANNAH
ON PONTOON SPANS

rison; but should I be forced to resort to assault, or the slower and surer process of Starvation, I shall then feel justified in resorting to the harshest measures, and shall make little effort to restrain my army—burning to avenge the national wrong which they attach to Savannah and to other large cities which have been so prominent in dragging our country into civil war. . . .

Hardee promptly turned Sherman down. The Federals, he contended, were at least four miles from central Savannah, and rather than being cut off he was "in free and constant communication" with his government. He would not be cowed by threats, he bluffed. What he was actually doing was masking his withdrawal.

Sherman reported the refusal to Grant, claiming, "General Hardee will learn whether I am right or not. . . . The route to which he refers, namely the Union plank-road, on the South Carolina shore, is inadequate to feed his Army and the people of Savannah." And Sherman repeated his desire "to have this Army turned loose on South Carolina," which would have "a direct and immediate bearing on your campaign in Virginia." Abruptly, he then left by sea for Hilton Head to persuade General Foster to use his troops to block Hardee's likely escape route, leaving behind instructions that Howard and Slocum were to maintain their siege of Savannah. Major Connolly cautioned as Sherman embarked that Foster, who was lame and used a crutch to get about, was "an old granny," too timid for strong action.

Although Hardee had already planned his next move, he needed time. A premature report was already circulating in Virginia, based apparently on Secretary Mallory's confidential orders to Hardee, that Savannah had either surrendered or was being evacuated. Major General Edward O. C. Ord telegraphed Grant, "A deserter from the 16th Georgia—in this morning[—]heard from a Doctor of the Regt who got it from the Lieut just from Richmond—who heard it from a member of the Cabinet night before last that Savannah had surrendered on the 16th, Genl Hardee having telegraphed he could not hold it—was directed to Evacuate."

While bluecoats built earthworks to accommodate six thirty-pound Parrott artillery pieces expected from Hilton Head, and tore up trackage to the south to prevent escape or reinforcement from that direction, Confederate recruits felled trees to block shallow swamps. They built more campfires than there were troops to gather round. To further distract the Federals, especially after dark, they swept the marshlands with grapeshot and fired hundreds of artillery rounds, rather plowing up mud than producing casualties. Expending ammunition that otherwise would have to be abandoned, or blown up, they were covering an engineering improvisation that would set them safely on the South Carolina bank of the broad Savannah.

Pickets posted close to each other exchanged barbs as well as bullets. Frederick Price, a New York recruit, wrote to his wife on December 18, "We have been here a week under dreadful fire from the enemy. We are so close to them that our men can talk with them." Bluecoats manning forward positions and suspecting some surprise called out in the darkness to the 5th Georgia Reserves, "Whatcha' doin' there, Johnny? Thought you was getting out tonight."

"We loves you too good, Yanks," came the reply as the Georgians quietly packed their gear. "We can't leave you." When the Federals warned that all Rebels standing their ground would be blown away, a Georgian challenged, "Blow up yer ass, Yank. Blow to hell!" Then the talking ceased.

Hoping to impede a Confederate withdrawal into South Carolina, Sherman conferred again with Foster at Hilton Head, urging the diffident general to "give his attention" to blocking the Union Causeway above King's Bridge. Outside the city, where Federal forces were taking hour after hour of shelling that suggested a large defensive buildup, Howard and Slocum impatiently awaited orders from their absent chief. In heavy rain after dark on the twentieth, Sherman and Hitchcock started back to Savannah with Admiral Dahlgren on his *Harvest Moon*. With the wind gusting strongly offshore, Dahlgren ordered his pilot to work his way to the Ogeechee indirectly through inland passages. The river fanned out into the Ossabaw Sound through myriad marshland waterways. "We were caught in a low tide," Sherman recalled, "and [became] stuck in the mud."

The only evidence at sea that something was happening in Savannah, Major John Gray wrote from shipboard, was "a dull red light" that shot up "into a tall fiery column with a ball of thick black smoke at its summit, and soon afterward we heard the explosion which shook the windows even at Hilton Head." The pyrotechnics were from the scuttling of the Rebel ram *Georgia*, which had been covering the withdrawal. Sherman could do nothing but guess at events.

When daylight came, sailors struggled to free *Harvest Moon*, yet only a high tide could lift it loose. Finally, Sherman recalled, the admiral "ordered out his barge; in it we pulled through this intricate and shallow channel, and toward evening of December 21st we discovered, coming toward us, a tug, called the *Red Legs*, . . . with a staff officer on board, bearing letters from Colonel Dayton to myself and the admiral, reporting that the city of Savannah had been found evacuated on the morning of December 21st, and was then in our possession. General Hardee['s army] had crossed the Savannah River by a pontoon-bridge, carrying off his men and light artillery, blowing up his iron-clads and navy-yard, and leaving for us all the heavy guns, stores, cotton, railway-cars, steamboats, and an immense amount of private property."

Sherman's memory was conveniently short. Hardee had obstructed the harbor for deep-draft ships with submerged pens of pilings filled with paving stones and rocks, and heavy iron chains. Most Rebel cannon had been spiked, ammunition and gunpowder dumped in canals and swamps, ships scuttled, forts rendered useless, and railway cars left without wheels. Yet a fortune in cotton remained intact in Savannah warehouses.

Dahlgren returned to Hilton Head on the *Sonoma*, which had followed from his blockading fleet. Sherman boarded the *Red Legs*, disembarked at King's Bridge, and rode ten miles to his camp. There he learned what had happened in his absence.

UNABLE TO AWAIT ORDERS to occupy Savannah, Slocum and Howard, with their staffs, were already there. To prevent disruption of life in the city, most troops were camped outside. Appropriately, it seemed, from Hardeeville, South Carolina, General Hardee (a native Georgian)* had already telegraphed to President Davis in Richmond, "On the 19th, the enemy forced a landing on the South Carolina side, so near my communications that to save the garrison it became necessary to give up the city. Its evacuation was successful. . . . Summed up, it was over 9,089." His count coolly excluded the hundreds of sick and wounded left behind, and the dozens of deserters "preferring to be made prisoners to fighting any longer," as Sergeant William Andrews explained, having taken advantage of the chaos in Savannah. "Doors were being knocked down, guns were firing in every direction, the bullets flying over and around us, Women and children screaming and rushing in every direction." Afterward, suddenly, there was quiet.

"Truly," General Howard conceded, "it was a small force to have given us so much trouble; but Savannah almost defended itself by its bays, bogs, and swamps all around, leaving only causeways to be defended." General Slocum had indeed landed a brigade across to the Carolina shore on the

---

* Hardeeville, once Purrysburg, was renamed for W. W. Hardee, a South Carolina businessman who had established Hardee's Station on the Charleston & Savannah Railroad.

nineteenth, which threatened the Union Causeway yet was impeded by a flooded rice plantation and the skirmishing of Joe Wheeler's ubiquitous cavalry. Thanks to Beauregard's initiative, Hardee had not counted on the causeway. Since December 9, John G. Clark, his dogged engineering officer, had supervised the assembly of small boats, barges, skiffs and rice flats (each flat about eighty feet long) to be lashed together in three segments by ropes and chains, and anchored by heavy rail car wheels disassembled from trains with nowhere to go. The makeshift bridge would be a mile long. One section was fixed into place at the foot of Broad Street and extended to the long sausage of Hutchinson's Island; the next extended to Pennyworth Island; and the final stage stretched to the South Carolina bank. Walls and flooring dismantled from nearby wharves and buildings were attached as a surface, and rice straw laid down to muffle the sounds of wagons and boots.

When Beauregard slipped in again on December 16 he was alarmed at the slow progress, but his energetic presence made a difference. Slaves, civilians, and soldiers completed the swaying spans after dark on the nineteenth. Civilians eager to escape were permitted to cross the next day. While the ironclad *Georgia*, which resembled a triangular rooftop on a barge, lobbed shells toward Federal emplacements along the river to keep prying eyes away, terrified townspeople who had assembled on Broad Street in a cold rain tried the narrow, daunting passage without rails, gingerly stumbled across on foot, and in wagons and carriages, then hurried toward Hardeeville, fifteen miles away. As a destination the hamlet left much to be desired. Joseph LeConte, an out-of-uniform Confederate explosives specialist and formerly a South Carolina professor, traveling by a circuitous route toward Walthourville (below Savannah) to avoid the Federals, described the backwater, soon to be overwhelmed with refugees, as "nothing but a railroad station with one commissary store-house by the roadside and two or three miserable huts in the pine wood."

At dusk, with Sherman still at sea, a more massive Rebel artillery bombardment erupted as the military phase of the evacuation began, still backlit hours later by the burning of the trapped gunboats *Isondiga*, *Firefly*, *Water Witch*, *Milledgeville*, and *Savannah* by their crews. Hardee and his staff had ferried off at 9:00 PM on the twentieth before the navy yard was wrecked. Despite the cover of Confederate shelling, muffled echoes from the evacuation could be heard from occupied islands in the Savannah to the South Carolina shore. Bluecoats of the 13th New Jersey upriver on Argyle Island listened to the shouts of teamsters urging across oxen pulling caissons. The retreating troops were even seen by some Federals, but orders were not to intervene. "A long detention [of prisoners]," O. O. Howard explained later, "would have been unfavorable to us in the opening of our next campaign."

In a gray mist that had followed a day of rain, forty-eight cannon on creaking carriages, and uncounted rumbling supply wagons, all that Hardee could procure, teetered across the floating spans along with the troops. One cannon pulled by a mule team tumbled into the river and was lost. Several baggage wagons tipped over and sank as the bridge swayed. Henry Lea Graves, a Confederate marine, would write to his mother, "I have no words to picture the gloomy bitterness that filled my breast on that dreary march through water, mud and darkness. . . . We started from the trenches at dark and reached the city at 12 o'clock midnight, halted an hour and fell into the long line of silent men who were pouring in a continuous stream over a pontoon bridge . . . [to] the Carolina shore."

A Rebel skirmish line near the bridge kept firing until 1:00 AM, when the rear guard began hurrying across. At 3:00 AM the last to leave were afoot. By 5:40 AM, engineers had detached the bridge segments and torched some of them. The smoking rubble drifted downstream as the rear guard scrambled ashore. Hardee would write after the war, "Although compelled to evacuate the city, there is no part of my military life to which I look back with so much satisfaction." With a scratch force of

CONFEDERATE DEFENDERS EVACUATING SAVANNAH
ACROSS A MAKESHIFT BRIDGE

little over 9,000 troops bolstered by some expert cannoneers, he had held off more than 60,000 seasoned Union soldiers while keeping Savannah relatively safe from the destruction wreaked upon other cities visited by Sherman's marchers through Georgia.

That the end for Savannah had come was still unknown in the North. Even for the Rebels, the *New York Times* editorialized, "we have good [holiday] wishes, and sincerely hope that Gen. Sherman will capture the fifteen thousand half starved Confederates shut up in Savannah, and give them all a Christmas dinner." The *Times*'s estimate of Hardee's troop strength, only a guess, was less inflated than that of most Federals mired on the siege lines.

ALTHOUGH CAMPFIRES STILL GLOWED within the earthworks of Savannah, the boom of cannon seemed now distant. Awakening in the sudden silence, Private Horatio Chapman of the Third Division's 20th Connecticut peered forward and saw a white cloth dangling from a stick. He called to his lieutenant and they cautiously went forward, finding two wounded Rebels abandoned by their comrades. "They're all gone but us," one said. "They pulled out in a big hurry."

As the first morning light on the twenty-first appeared on the eastern horizon, Colonel Barnum of the Second Division's 3rd Brigade sent search squads into the city. They found the streets empty and the last of Hardee's troops disappearing into the gray mist across the river. Federals now learning of the evacuation climbed out of their tents in dress and undress, most of them shouting hurrahs. "The Johnnys got out last night," Private Upson wrote with little disappointment when he heard that the Savannah force had slipped away. "I think our officers knew they were going and did not try to stop them for we could hear them all night moving about and most of us think if we had pushed the fighting on our right front a little harder we might have cut them off and captured the whole of them." Yet he added, "I am awfully glad we didn't have to charge their works for we would have lost a good many lives, that's sure."

AT DAWN, Brigadier General John Geary (a major general a month later) and Colonel Henry Barnum led a brigade of New Yorkers and Pennsylvanians from Geary's Second Division into Savannah. Barnum could hardly believe he was there. As a major at Malvern Hill in Virginia in July 1862 he had been severely wounded and left for dead. To surrender the undefended city, Mayor Richard Arnold and those aldermen who had not fled met the first Federals near a railroad junction on the Augusta Road. The city officials were on foot; Confederate stragglers had stolen their horses. "Where resistance is hopeless," Arnold said, "it is criminal to make it." He brought a letter for Sherman:

> Sir, The city of Savannah was last night evacuated by the Confederate military and is now entirely defenseless. As chief

magistrate of the city I respectfully request your protection of
the lives and private property of the citizens and of our women
and children.

The *Richmond Dispatch* editorialized, with utter nastiness, "An Arnold was the solitary traitor of the old Revolution. An Arnold is the first person in this [one] who has basely gone over to the enemy."

At first light, Barnum's Third Brigade began marching down West Broad Street to Bay Street, unfurling the Stars and Stripes from the dome of the Exchange and over the Customs House. The morning issue of the *Savannah Republican*, the last printed before Union occupation, announced on its front page,

> To the citizens of Savannah
>
> By the fortunes of war we pass today under the authority of the Federal military authorities. The evacuation of Savannah by the Confederate army, which took place last night has left the gates of the city open, and Gen. Sherman with his army will no doubt to-day take possession. We desire to counsel obedience and all proper respect on the part of our citizens, and to express belief that our property and persons will be respected by our military rulers. . . . It behooves all to keep within their houses until Gen. Sherman can organize a provost system. Let our conduct be such as to win the admiration of a magnanimous foe, and give no ground for complaint or harsh treatment on the part of him who will for an indefinite period hold possession of our city.

The rogue element in Savannah, however, did not read newspapers. Rebel stragglers, deserters, and local scum, as in Atlanta—and in all wars—rushed to seize what could be carried away. Geary's provost guard soon quieted the city while Slocum and Howard moved in with their headquarters staffs. A former mayor of San Francisco, John Geary was efficient and tough. "It was fortunate," Major Nichols wrote, "that our troops followed so quickly . . . , for a mob had gathered in the streets, and were breaking into the stores and [ware]houses. They were with difficulty dispersed by the bayonets of our soldiers, and then, once more, order and confidence prevailed throughout. . . ."

The *Boston Evening Transcript*'s correspondent agreed, reporting that although the interval between retreat and occupation was brief, "it was long enough to enable the worst passions of the populace to break loose and show themselves in acts of wanton destruction and indiscriminate plunder of stores and warehouses. Upon the business streets the work of wholesale burglary was going on at such a rate . . . in 'tearing down and dragging out,' that old citizens have expressed to me their convictions that a delay of another half hour on the part of our troops would have witnessed the conflagration of the whole city, at the hands of its own inhabitants."

THE NAVY YARD AND
FLOATING BATTERY *SAVANNAH* AFIRE

Ironically, Savannah on surrender was initially spared Sherman. His unanticipated delay at sea meant that his team of Howard, Slocum, and Geary quickly established the civil parameters of possession. Order and decorum prevailed. Sherman entered less as a commander rather aloof to campaigning excesses he often excused away, than as managing director of the ongoing business of occupation. "The People here seem to be well content as they have reason to be," Sherman would write to Grant, "for our troops have behaved magnificently. You would think it Sunday, so quiet is Every thing in the city day & night."

Early on December 22, Sherman recalled, "I moved in with my own headquarters, and rode down Bull Street to the custom-house, from the roof of which we had an extensive view over the city, the river, and the vast extent of marsh, and rice-fields on the South Carolina side. The navy-yard, and the wreck of the iron-clad ram CSS *Georgia*, were still smouldering, but all else looked quiet enough." Among the last evacuees had been the crewmen of the scuttled *Georgia*. Iverson Dutton Graves, brother of Henry Graves, a marine already ashore in South Carolina, wrote home a month later, "I buckled on my armor, made a little knapsack, put in two changes of clothes, strapped on a blanket and shawl. . . . The Yankees were kind enough to stop the shelling, . . . so we effected a landing on the South Carolina shore in small boats without molestation. We were about six miles distance when our ship blew up, and you have no idea what a sad blow it was to me. Thinks I, there goes my pleasant quarters, my good clothes, my warm overcoat, and I am forever cut off from Savannah and the hope of making myself agreeable to the Sav. girls." But he had been "provident enough" to fill his canteen from the ship's store of whiskey, and once ashore, "taking a good swig, I felt the generous fluid to course through every vein and fill me with fresh strength and spirit."

At the Pulaski Hotel, the prime guesthouse, which Sherman scouted as temporary quarters, he found that he knew the proprietor, a Vermonter once a clerk at the St. Louis Hotel in New Orleans. With no likelihood of his usual clientele, the ex-Yankee was eager to have Sherman stay, "but soon I explained to him that we had a full mess equipment along, and that we were not in the habit of paying board." While Sherman considered keeping a wing of the hotel for his headquarters, and dispatched an aide to look for a livery stable, Mayor Arnold walked into the hotel to pay his respects. With him were a brother of General Hardee and Charles Green, an elderly and wealthy British cotton merchant from Liverpool long resident in Savannah. Green said that he had a fine home nearby and would require only a few rooms for himself should Sherman wish to use it. General Howard, Green explained, had told him the day before that it would be appropriate, and its use would not subject a Southerner to any perceived indignity.

"At first I felt strongly disinclined to make use of any private dwelling," Sherman recalled, "lest complaints should arise of damage and loss of furniture, and so expressed myself to Green; but after riding about the city, and finding his house so spacious, so convenient, with a large yard and stabling, I accepted his offer." The mansion on Madison Square, Major Hitchcock wrote to his wife, Mary, had been "very handsomely furnished *before the war*—looks a little worn now. In the wide hall are some . . . pieces of statuary, banana trees growing in tubs, etc., and several fine pictures in the various rooms. . . ." Sherman explained to Ellen that his elegant bath, dressing room and bedroom "look out of proportion to my poor baggage."

As his immediate staff moved in, an unexpected visitor turned up. Alfred Gallatin Browne, a Treasury agent from Port Royal charged with supervising commerce and seizing Rebel goods in occupied areas of the Confederacy, had arrived on the ship carrying the army's backlog of mail, and began claiming "all captured cotton, rice, buildings, etc. Having use for these articles ourselves, and having fairly earned them, I did not feel inclined to surrender possession, and explained to him that the quartermaster and commissary could manage them more to our liking than he; but I agreed, after the proper inventories had been prepared, if there remained any thing for which we had no special use, I would turn it over to him."

A preliminary inspection indicated that at least 25,000 bales of cotton were in city warehouses, and abandoned coastal forts had at least 150 heavy guns.* "At that interview, Mr. Browne, who was a shrewd, clever Yankee [from Salem, Massachusetts], told me that he was . . . starting for Old Point Comfort, [at Hampton, Virginia]." Since with good weather at sea he would reach Fortress Monroe there by Christmas, "he suggested that I might make it the occasion of sending a welcome Christmas gift to the President, Mr. Lincoln, who peculiarly enjoyed such pleasantry."

Sherman seized the moment. On "a slip of paper" he wrote a message to be left at the telegraph office at Fortress Monroe for transmission† to the Executive Mansion:

> December 22, 1864
> To His Excellency President Lincoln, Washington, D.C.:
> I beg to present you as a Christmas-gift the city of
> Savannah, with one hundred and fifty heavy guns and plenty
> of ammunition, also about twenty-five thousand bales of
> cotton.
>
> W. T. Sherman,
> Major-General

---

* Later tallies increased the cotton total to 31,000 and coastal artillery seized to more than 250 pieces.
† Because Lee's presence in Virginia blocked direct wires to Washington, a cable under Chesapeake Bay furnished the means to transmit messages circuitously.

EIGHT

Savannah Christmas

S HERMAN'S TELEGRAM ARRIVED AT THE WHITE
House on Christmas Eve, the day that troops of the
two Federal wings were being encamped around,
rather than within, Savannah, while orderly life in the city was
restored. The President responded on the day after Christmas,
his message carried south by walrus-mustached Major General John A. Logan, veteran of Vicksburg and Atlanta, who
would be taking over XV Corps from Peter Osterhaus. Logan
had been given leave by Sherman to return to Illinois to use
his considerable political influence to campaign for Lincoln.

Executive Mansion
Washington, D.C.
Dec. 26, 1864

My Dear General Sherman,
    Many, many thanks for your Christmas gift—
the capture of Savannah.

When you were about to leave Atlanta for the Atlantic coast, I was anxious, if not fearful; but feeling that you were the better judge, and remembering that "nothing risked nothing gained," I did not interfere. Now, the undertaking being a success, the honor is all yours, for I believe none of us went further than to acquiesce. And taking the work of General Thomas* into the count, as it should be taken, it is indeed a great success.

Not only does it afford the obvious and immediate military advantages, but in showing to the world that your army could be divided, putting the stronger part to an important new service, and yet leaving enough to vanquish the old opposing forces of the whole—Hood's army—it brings those who sat in darkness to see a great light.

But what next? I suppose it will be safe if I leave General Grant and yourself to decide.

Please make my grateful acknowledgments to your whole army, officers and men.

Yours very truly,

A. Lincoln

In Washington early that morning, a thunderous salute of two hundred guns was fired to mark the capture of Savannah. Sherman's telegram had made him an instant hero in the North. Although the message

---

* Augmented by troops sent north to Tennessee by Sherman, Major General George H. Thomas had defeated the troops of John Bell Hood at Nashville December 15–18, forcing the Confederate remnants to retreat south and disappear as a factor in the war. A follow-up witticism to Sherman's message appeared in the press that Thomas's Christmas present to the "wayward sisters"—the Rebel states—was a "worsted Hood."

"SANTA CLAUS SHERMAN PUTTING
SAVANNAH INTO UNCLE SAM'S STOCKING"

was hardly the general's own idea, as he later conceded, it was received
as a grand imaginative gesture. The *Chicago Tribune* called him, in a
headline, "Our Military Santa Claus." *Frank Leslie's Illustrated Newspaper*
published a cartoon picturing Sherman stuffing the city of Savannah
in Uncle Sam's Christmas stocking. Signing his telegram "Your Friend,
U. S. Grant," Sherman's superior on the Virginia front wired congratulations on concluding a "most brilliant campaign . . . the like of which is
not read of in past history. I never had a doubt of the result. . . . I would

not have entrusted the expedition to any other living commander." Anticipating nationwide enthusiasm, Assistant Secretary of the Treasury Hugh McCulloch telegraphed, "Our joy was irrepressible. . . . It was an assurance that the days of the Confederacy were numbered. Every member of the Cabinet knew, at last, that the war was won and the Union safe." A New Hampshire paper published a "Christmas hymn" to Sherman, that thanks to him, the "old flag" flew again from Savannah's rooftops. Newspapers were flooded with Christmas verses and songs of dubious merit about Sherman's Yuletide "gift." In a flight of inspiration, a composer of a Christmas hymn ingeniously rhymed "Hosannah" with Savannah.

Summing up the campaign later, Sherman judged that his troops had done whatever they were called upon to do "with alacrity and a degree of cheerfulness unsurpassed. A little loose in foraging, they 'did some things they ought not to have done,' yet on the whole they have supplied the wants of the army with as little violence as could have been expected, and as little loss as I calculated." The festive images persisted. "Without an exception," the correspondent from the *Boston Evening Transcript* wrote from Savannah, "all speak of the march from Atlanta to this place as if it were one grand continuous holiday excursion." In the entire command, the army, marching three hundred miles in twenty-four days, had (by official account) lost 5 officers and 58 men killed, with 13 officers and 232 men wounded. One officer and 258 men remained missing, most of them likely dead—snatched or lost during bummer forays.

Sherman estimated, too, that of twenty thousand or more black "contrabands" who had left their masters, more than six thousand had clung to his columns all the way to Savannah and needed food and shelter. Fortunately, he did not have to feed and sequester the Confederate troops who had crossed into the Carolinas. It was enough to oversee the 986 prisoners captured during the march and take custody of the 1,200 sick and wounded Rebels Hardee had abandoned.

To Sherman's north, another Union campaign along the Atlantic coast was going badly—as much a fiasco as Savannah had been a success. Seizure of the North Carolina port of Wilmington had been stalled for more than a year by the diversion of resources toward blockaded Rebel Charleston. Finally, late in 1864, Sherman's friend from the Vicksburg siege, Rear Admiral David Dixon Porter, assembled more than 60 warships and troop transports, with 6,500 infantrymen under the blowhard Benjamin Franklin Butler of Massachusetts, to attack Fort Fisher, below Wilmington. A political major general, Butler's clout at home had been considered critical to Lincoln's reelection. Henry Halleck had long deplored giving Butler any command whatever as "little better than murder." More than a few of the 583 Union generals commissioned during the war were ineffective party stalwarts.

For reducing Fort Fisher, Butler conceived the strategy of loading an old ship with 350 tons of gunpowder, running it into nearby shallows, and shattering the garrison with the explosion. Atlantic storms had delayed the operation until Christmas Eve, when the timed fuse on the obsolete *Louisiana*, towed by the *Wilderness* close to the shore, failed. A volunteer crew set fire to the stern of the mined ship and escaped before the *Louisiana* detonated, ringing the ears of Fort Fisher's defenders. Unaware of Butler's scheme, the Rebel commander noted laconically in his diary, "A blockader got aground near the fort, set fire to herself and blew up."

At 10:48 AM on Christmas Day, Admiral Porter's fleet closed in again and renewed its bombardment. Most shells landed on the earthworks or in the Cape Fear River. A few hit heavy batteries, and two formidable 7-inch Brooke rifles cast by the Tredegar foundry in Richmond exploded. "I never saw shells fall so thick," a Confederate in the garrison recalled. "They came down like hail. I thought every shell would get us. We did not enjoy Christmas." Nor did the assault troops. Although warships trying to force a passage were blocked by a sandbar and driven

UNION TROOPS ASHORE TO ATTACK FORT FISHER

back by heavy fire, Butler put two thousand Federals ashore north of the fort. As the weather worsened in the late afternoon he ordered a withdrawal. Battered by heavy seas, more than seven hundred troops were left on the beach, covered by supporting fire from the Union *Santiago de Cuba*. It would take until December 27 to evacuate the desperate and sodden men.

General Butler returned to Virginia expecting the worst. Prodded by Porter's wire urging Butler's removal, Grant called the expedition "a gross and culpable failure." With no further political need of Butler in New England, Lincoln relieved him of his command.*

Grant had his own nautical frustrations at Christmas. His teenage son Fred came to spend his holiday at City Point, arriving with his mother's cousin, Will Smith. "Altogether I think he will have a good

---

* A week later a reconstituted force of eight thousand soldiers, sailors, and marines under a more effective general, Alfred Terry, smothered Fort Fisher with gunfire and stormed the fort, taking two thousand prisoners.

time of it while he stays here," Grant wrote to his wife. But bored at the general's headquarters cabin, and with arranged introductions to army bigwigs, Fred and Will went duck hunting on the James River. As they paddled, the boy wearing his suspiciously gray school uniform, a Union river patrol took them into custody as Confederate spies. It required earnest convincing that Fred was the son of the general in chief before the pair were released.

GENERAL SHERMAN had hardly occupied his quarters in Charles Green's mansion when lady petitioners from Savannah's elite began queuing at his door. The spouses of Confederate generals Gustavus Smith, Lafayette McLaws, William Hardee, and A. P. Stewart came with letters from their husbands asking for his personal interest in the welfare of their families. "Dear Sherman," the plea from General Smith of the Georgia Militia began, "The fortunes of war compel me to leave my wife in Savannah, and I beg for her courteous protection." Sherman visited her later "and saw, personally, that she had no reason to complain." He advised Mrs. Stewart, whose husband commanded a corps in Hood's army, to return north to her family home in Cincinnati, where her uncle was a judge. Mrs. Sarah Davidson also appealed for protection, explaining that she had three sons in the Union army, three sons with Confederate units in the South, and a son-in-law serving in Virginia with Lee.

"The women here are . . . disposed to usurp my time more from curiosity than business," Sherman wrote to Ellen, for he expected his provost marshal to keep the lid on troop excesses. "They have been told of my burning and killing until they expected the veriest monster, but their eyes were opened when . . . the three chief officers of the Rebel Army fled across the Savannah River, consigning their families to my special care. There are some very elegant people here whom I knew in better days and who do not seem ashamed to call on the 'Vandal Chief.' They regard us just as the Romans did the Goths and the parallel is not unjust. Many of my men with red beards and stalwart frames look like giants."

Another petitioner, an elegantly dressed gentleman, hurried to see the general early in the occupation. His sartorial opposite, Sherman (according to one observer) wore a "black felt hat slouched over the eyes, . . . dirty dickey with the points wilted down, black, old-fashioned stock, brown field officer's coat with high collar and no shoulder straps, muddy trowsers and one spur." Sherman had observed British flags flying from buildings discovered to be warehousing cotton, and ordered seizure of the bales. All the cotton, Edmund Molyneux explained in polite indignation, "was protected by the British flag." It had been purchased by British merchants, and he had the bills to prove it.

"Stop, sir," said Sherman, "not your cotton, sir, but *my* cotton, in the name of the United States Government, sir."

"But, sir, there is scarcely any cotton in Savannah that does not belong to me."

"There is not a pound of cotton here, sir, that does not belong to me, for the United States."

"Well, sir, my Government shall hear of this. I shall report your conduct to my Government, sir!"

"Ah! Pray, who are you, sir?" Sherman asked.

"Consul to Her British Majesty, sir!" His superior in Washington was the British Minister, Sir Richard Lyons, who had needed all his considerable diplomatic skills since 1861 to keep the two nations from overt war.

"Oh, indeed! I hope you will report me to your Government. If British subjects paid for that cotton, I know what they purchased it for. They gave the Rebels powder, lead, shot and cannon for it. You will please say to your Government, for me, that I have been fighting the English Government all the way from the Ohio River to Vicksburg, and thence to this point. At every step I have encountered British arms, British munitions of war, and British goods of every description—at every step, sir. I have met them, sir, in all shapes,* and now, sir, I find you claiming all the cotton, sir. . . . The names of any claimants will be taken; . . . and be probably the subject of future action; but there the matter must rest for the present. Good day, sir."

Over the consul's protests, General Howard had set up his headquarters in Molyneux's classic revival-style mansion on Bull Street. Assuming the consul's diplomatic immunity, some Savannah citizens had stockpiled their finest liquors "under the protection of the British flag" in one locked room and other valuables in another room. Howard, however, pocketed all the keys, which he entrusted to Captain Wimer Bedford of his staff, who recalled, "We did not much care for the British flag." Bedford knew where some Rebel equipment used against them had originated. "We had no respect therefore for the English Government and hence none for its flag." The Molyneux family claimed after the war that $10,000 worth of goods and furnishings (a great deal then in purchasing power) had been unlawfully removed by the Federals.

THE CORRESPONDENT of the *Boston Evening Transcript* claimed that "a sullen acquiescence in what seemed an inevitable fate, was the only visible emotion on the part of the white inhabitants. . . . If we except the foreigners and the negroes, I very much doubt if there is any larger number of Union men [resident] in Savannah than there were righteous ones in Sodom, and I do not believe that the generous sympathy and liberality of the North will have any effect upon their obdurate hearts." Deterrent

---

* In the most recent incident, on December 9, Major Thomas Osborn's artillerymen had disabled and captured two "Blakely guns just imported from England. . . . The shipper's mark in white paint on the guns and carriages was not [yet] soiled." The huge air-chambered, rifled guns fired 700-pound projectiles. The powerful weapons had slipped through the blockade.

shows of Federal strength contributed to the enmity. Although Saturday, December 24, was cold and windy, troops encamped outside Savannah began marching into the city, unit by unit, to remind residents how substantial the occupation was, and to give soldiers an opportunity to see the target of their campaign. Some plucked white camellias from local gardens to stick in their hats.

Sherman's headquarters staffs were efficient at settling in. Men whose enlistments had expired during the march, or who were retrieved prisoners (nearly three hundred had reached Union lines), were processed for home. Private S. J. Gibson of the 103rd Pennsylvania Volunteers had his pay brought up to date, was given $36.00, and shipped out on Christmas Eve. Marching sprightly to the Green mansion, the band of the 33rd Massachusetts serenaded Sherman with "Home, Sweet Home," followed by "When This Cruel War Is Over" and "Rally Round the Flag." Carols were not yet customary in America. "O Little Town of Bethlehem" was written and composed in Philadelphia in 1867–1868.

The next day was Christmas, and a Sunday. Speaking on behalf of several local preachers, a clergyman asked Sherman cautiously, as Geary reported it, "Well, General, the diocese of Georgia requires us to pray for certain persons. Will that be objectionable?"

"Yes, certainly, pray for Jeff Davis," Sherman agreed. "Certainly pray for the Devil, too. I don't know any two that require prayers more than they do." (Although the invocation for President Davis would be quietly omitted, the remark was widely quoted in the Northern press.)

Local officeholders from mayor to lower functionaries were kept on duty, as long as they did not interfere with the Union occupation, and Sherman ordered farmer's markets to remain open so that people could find food. Confederate currency, however, was now nearly worthless. Since bundles of it were needed for purchases, local shops began offering paper Rebel dollars for five Union cents. Troops permitted into Savannah bought fistfuls to use for poker. Private John Peters happily noted winning at cards one hundred dollars—probably of the discounted five-cent variety. Private Frederick Buerstatte noted in his laconic diary, "We cleaned our quarters. Each person planted a Christmas tree in front of his tent." Very likely no soldier with access to an ax paid anyone anything for his tree, but provost marshal patrols now watched over Savannah's shade trees.

WHERE THE FEDERALS HAD COME through earlier, Christmas Eve was bleak. On the large spread of Argyle Island in the Savannah River, the Gowrie rice plantation of Louis Manigault, a wealthy Charleston slave owner with several lucrative holdings, was sacked the day before Christmas. Every building was burned to the ground except the eleven brick dwellings of Manigault's blacks. Ten thousand bushels of rice were confiscated, along with all the mules, and the estate's towering water oaks were felled for firewood.

To the west, Eliza and Metta Andrews, daughters of Judge Garnett Andrews, who lived near Augusta, had been sent toward the apparent safety of their elder sister's plantation in southwest Georgia. In their twenties, the sisters were capable of traveling on their own, but transport in burned-out middle Georgia was not easy. Few trains ran, or could proceed very far, and a ride on a springless plantation wagon with no backs to the seats, and no roof, required an exorbitant fee. In a week, by December 24, they reached Macon. Confederate discipline was crumbling. They had encountered "crowds" of soldiers moving aimlessly in both directions: "It was like traveling through the streets of a populous town all day. They were mostly on foot, and I saw numbers seated on the roadside greedily eating raw turnips, meat skins, parched corn—anything they could find, even picking up the loose grain that Sherman's horses had left."

Before crossing the Oconee toward Milledgeville on an improvised ferry where Federals had burned the bridge, the Andrews women came to a field "where 30,000 Yankees had camped hardly three weeks before. It was strewn with the *débris* they had left behind, and the poor people of the neighborhood were wandering over it, seeking for anything they could find to eat. . . . We were told that a great many valuables were found there at first, plunder that the invaders had left . . . , but the place had been picked over so often by this time that little now remained except tufts of loose cotton, piles of half-rotted grain, and the carcasses of slaughtered animals, which raised a horrible stench." Still, farmers were stubbornly plowing at one end of the field, to make ready for next year's crops. The women continued through Milledgeville and Gordon, where the railroad track "was torn up and the iron twisted into every conceivable shape, Some of it was wrapped around the trunks of trees. . . ."*

When a working railway station on an embankment appeared in view, it was "in the midst of a big swamp, with crowds of people waiting on little knolls and islands till the cars should be opened." It "looked like a gypsy camp." Eliza and Metta boarded the next train, which clattered to a stop two miles from Macon, at a damaged and weakened bridge. Eliza wept. At ten on Christmas Eve a panting engine and single boxcar arrived at the other end of the eighty-foot-high trestle over Walnut Creek. They walked unsteadily across into Christmas.

* * *

---

* In October 1866 the *Richmond Dispatch* reported that 800 tons of mangled rails were received at the Tredegar Iron Works, which had been the Confederacy's major arms supplier. "The rails were some of those destroyed by Sherman's Raid, and some were tied in a bow-knot, and in the centre of one coil of iron bar was the trunk of a tree, around which it had been wrapped. The iron will be worked up again into rails."

ON CHRISTMAS DAY, Hitchcock wrote, "the churches—at least five or six principal ones—were open as usual and going with the General to St. John's (Episcopal) across the street, I was delighted to see it filled, not only by a large number of our officers and men, but also a considerable number of Savannah people, ladies and gentlemen." At a Baptist service, an Iowan estimated that a thousand soldiers attended. Because of the army component at St. John's, and Sherman's presence, a Union chaplain assisted. Hitchcock was amused that "when the minister came to the prayer for the President of the United States"—the books in the pews were obviously prewar—"he simply omitted that prayer altogether and passed directly on from the preceding one to the Litany without pause." Sherman's remark had given Savannah preachers pause, including the Rev. Cameron McRae, who with his wife had resided with Charles Green. "My honored guest for some years past," said Green, introducing the clergyman to Sherman, who had taken over the couple's rooms, leaving them to find other lodgings.

Frances Thomas Howard, a Southerner devoted to the Confederacy, observed some parishioners leaving, in implicit rejection of the Federal presence, without "partaking of the sacrament. This has been a sorrowful Christmas Day." The unrelenting snobbery and obvious hostility of most churchgoing women in their prewar silks and trappings that Christmas irritated a Minnesota private, who wrote home that "they came out, more to Show them Selves than for the good of there Never dieing Souls. Which Should of been the main object of attending Divine Servis."

To her sister in New York, a much different sort of Savannah woman, unidentified in a press account in the North, wrote, "This morning I went to St. John's Church. Mr. McRae preached. He did not read the prayer for

"CHRISTMAS DAY IN SAVANNAH—
GENERAL SHERMAN'S CHRISTMAS DINNER AT MR. GREEN'S"

the President of the United States, but [said he] will next Sunday.* All
the churches were open today except Christ's Church. The Bishop left.
I hope it will be open on Sunday [next], for I shall take great pleasure in
seeing a Union man in the pulpit. The Bishop [also] sent off his assistant
before he left. What fools some people have been; they will see their folly

---

* He did not. According to the *Boston Evening Transcript*, "None of the white
  ministers pray for the President, but the black ones supplicate heartily for him
  and the Government. A Presbyterian minister prayed . . . 'For all Presidents,
  that their minds might be illuminated to see the right and following it, eschew-
  ing the wrong,' which was just as much for Jeff. Davis as for A. Lincoln."

when too late, I fear. Last evening I sent General Sherman a Christmas present. May God bless him. . . ."

She felt especially blessed by having quartered "next door" a company of New York Volunteers. Her maid, Sarah, presumably a slave on the edge of freedom, took "a great delight in making coffee for them. . . . I have a picket walking up and down before my door all day and night to guard me, and they take the best care of me." She had even made them a flag. The Third Brigade of the 2nd Division had lost its colors in a fire and had none on entry into Savannah. "Each division has a flag—1st, red star; 2d, white star, and 3d blue. So I made the bonnie blue flag with the single white star, and there is not one of the men but knows it and seems perfectly delighted. . . . I am the happiest woman in Savannah."

She reported enjoying, with company, "a glorious Christmas dinner. I suppose you wonder what we could have. I will tell you. I bought two pairs of turkeys a few days since, for which I paid $85 a pair. I had two of these roasted, a splendid chicken pie, cold slaw, celery, sweet potatoes, turnips, champagne, apple pie, pumpkin pie, oranges, pecan nuts, &c; so we did very well considering. But if I had not had plenty of Confederate bills to pay for all I would have been rather hard up for a Christmas dinner. When I heard that General Sherman said he would eat his Christmas dinner in Savannah, I felt sure he would. There are many here who did not believe he would come, and made no preparation. The country all around is bare. . . ."

Harper's Weekly for December 31 would publish an imaginary "Union Christmas Dinner" by Thomas Nast showing President Lincoln welcoming the chilled and chastened Rebels into the White House. In Savannah on Christmas evening, Sherman convened in the Green mansion what he described in a letter home as a "family dinner party"—his military family.* George Ward Nichols of the staff had secured turkeys for roasting "and sundry other good things," as Hitchcock put it, and Henry Barnum, soon to be promoted to brigadier general, brought "some very good wine presented to him by some wine-merchants here at whose shops he placed a guard immediately on our troops entering the city." Charles Green's china and silver were "kindly loaned for the occasion," and he was the only civilian guest of the twenty at the table. Although Sherman presided, dinner began with a toast to him by a colleague, and he "made a little speech, patriotic, modest, and pointed." Green made "as happy a little after-dinner speech as I ever heard–Gen. S. proposing his health." Hitchcock "withdrew quietly soon after the toasts began[,] fearing a little I confess, that they might become too lively, but in that I was mistaken." From his second-floor room over the hall, with a bow window overlooking the street, he wrote a Christmas letter to his wife.

Sherman's peculiarly capitalized Christmas letter to Ellen vowing his "Eternal affection" boasted that Confederate die-hards "no longer Call my army 'Cowardly yanks' but have tried to arouse the Sympathy of the civilized world by stories of the cruel barbarities of my Army. The next stop in the progress will be 'for gods sake Spare us, we must surrender'—when that end is reached we begin to See daylight, but although I have come right through the heart of Georgia, they talk as defiantly as ever. I think Thomas' whipping [Hood] at Nashville, coupled with my march will take Some conceit out of them." He found it difficult to contain his pride under a cloak of modesty, closing, "I have no doubt you hear enough about 'Sherman' and are sick of the name, and the interest the public takes in my whereabouts leaves me no subject to write about." He also wrote to General Thomas, "I do not believe your own wife was more happy at the results [in Tennessee] than I was."

---

* *Harper's Weekly* on January 28, 1865, would publish a half-page illustration of its war artist's "Christmas Day in Savannah—Sherman's Christmas Dinner."

* * *

THE FREED BLACKS who swelled the population of Savannah were an awkward presence for Sherman. He employed the sturdiest males as wage laborers, but all had to be fed and clothed, and somehow settled without antagonizing local whites. Although to Major John Chipman Gray, who saw the general in Savannah, Sherman was "tall and lank, . . . with hair like thatch, which he rubs up with his hands, a rusty beard trimmed close, a wrinkled face, sharp prominent red nose, small, bright eyes, [and] coarse red hands," he was godlike to the throngs of former slaves who clustered in Madison Square, the small public park opposite the Green residence, for a sight of him, or to appeal for an audience

SHERMAN'S HEADQUARTERS
IN THE GREEN MANSION, SAVANNAH

with him. Henry Hitchcock would write to Mary that from the day of Sherman's arrival:

> There was a constant stream of them, old and young, men, women and children, black, yellow and cream-colored, uncouth and well-bred, bashful and talkative—but always respectful and well-behaved—all day long, anxious to pay their respects and to see the man they had heard so much of, and whom—as more than one told him—God had sent as an answer to their prayers. Frequently they came in a dozen or twenty at a time, to his room up-stairs where he usually sits. . . . He has always shown them in at once, stopping a dispatch or letter or conversation to greet them in his off-hand—though not undignified way—"Well, boys—come to see Mr. Sherman, have you! Well, I'm Mr. Sherman—glad to see you!"—and shaking hands with them all. . . . Almost all of them who have talked at all have spoken of our success and their deliverance with an apparently religious feeling—"Been prayin' for you all long time, Sir, prayin' day and night for you, and, bless God, you is come" etc. One old preacher likened himself to Simeon of old, kindly reminding the General of the particulars as given in the Gospel.

"It would amuse you," Sherman wrote to Ellen that Christmas, "to See the negros, they flock to me old & young[,] they pray & shout—and mix up my name with that of Moses, & Simon, and other scriptural ones as well as Abram Linkum the Great Messiah of 'Dis Jubilee.'" Sherman himself was slightly mixed up, as the Messiah-focused elderly black preacher was probably thinking of the "just and devout" elder in Jerusalem who, in the Gospel of Luke, greeted the infant Jesus in the Temple.

* * *

LITTLE MORE THAN two hundred of the city's residents were Jewish. Those of military age were in Confederate service. Major Samuel Yates Levy of the 1st Georgia Volunteers had been taken prisoner in June and was in the stockade at Johnson's Island. Octavus S. Cohen, Jr., a lieutenant at seventeen in 1863, was a brigade ordnance officer in South Carolina. Early on the afternoon on the first day of the occupation, General Howard's staff came to the gracious Cohen corner residence on Lafayette Square in search of quarters. In the four-page surviving fragment of her diary, Fanny Yates Cohen, one of the most obstreperous of Savannah's many hostile women, wrote that the Union men, "liking the appearance of our house," gave the family until five that afternoon to vacate it. The prospect of eviction did not improve her Rebel disposition.

When her father, Octavus Cohen, a commission merchant and cotton exporter, protested "that there were ladies in the house and it would be exceedingly inconvenient to move them out," one of Howard's officers remarked belligerently, "Well! I suppose *it will inconvenience* you but you know you Rebs *will* fight and when you are Conquered you must submit to whatever will contribute to our comfort." Diplomatically, Cohen offered them his stable for their horses, and recommended a vacated residence across the street. (Rather, Howard would occupy the Consul Molyneux mansion.) But for firewood stolen from their property and the flight of Harry, one of the Cohen "house servants," their lives were only briefly interrupted.

Fanny had been advised that if the family needed assistance of any sort she should apply to Orlando Poe, and on December 23, Sherman's chief engineer called. Although she had asked for his good offices, she wrote as if he had intruded: "I was obliged to receive him and never was so embarrassed in my life. My hatred for the Army in which he was an officer and my desire to be polite made me almost speechless—the contending feelings were more than I could control. He, however, conducted himself like a gentleman and offered us all the assistance in his power, but . . . we know our turn must soon come and we should be compelled to have some brute in our house who would make our life more miserable than it already was."

On Christmas Eve, Captain Gilbert Dunbar, General Kilpatrick's quartermaster, came asking for her father. Kilpatrick's reputation poisoned the courteous Dunbar's visit. Kilpatrick was obviously seeking quarters and was far more a potential horror than "Old Prayer Book" Howard. As Octavus Cohen was out, Fanny received Dunbar "standing up so that he could have no excuse for remaining longer than his business required him to do. I told him he could probably have our front parlor, but as my father was out could not give him a positive answer; in a couple of hours he returned and asked to see me again. I went down to him and he told me the order had been countermanded and he should not require the room. I told him I was glad that we were relieved. . . . " As he left she "opened the front door for him and he walked out like a well bred dog. . . ."

Later in the day, General Hazen visited in search of quarters. The Cohen family had known him well before the war when he was stationed in Savannah, but "this man" was now the enemy. "We have been forced to give him two rooms," Fanny wrote unrepentantly. It would be "a hard trial but I suppose we must submit." He was to occupy the parlor and a guest room, but delayed his arrival until early in the new year, having supervised the destruction of trackage on the Gulf Railroad south to Walthourville. Yet the "anticipation" was enough to make Fanny feel "prematurely old." She was twenty-four.

On Christmas Day, not her family's special holiday, she wrote, nevertheless, "This is the saddest Christmas that I have ever spent and my only pleasure during the day has been in looking forward to spending my next Christmas in the Confederacy. This morning my uncle . . . told us of a party given the evening before by the Negroes of Genl. Geary's Hd Qrts when the Gen went into the kitchen and desired an introduction to the *ladies* and *gentlemen* there assembled." (Very likely the "party" was an impromptu Christmas celebration by the kitchen staff.) Geary "asked who were slaves and who were free. There was but one slave present, a servant girl of my Aunt's, who acknowledged the fact. This elegant gentleman enquired into her private history and finding that she was a married woman . . . , presented [her husband], as a Christmas gift, with a *free wife*. The girl was so much amused, having always been a favorite servant and treated like one of the family, that she told it to her mistress as a good joke." What the young slave did not realize was that by authority of Lincoln's Emancipation Proclamation she was already legally free, as were all chattels in Confederate territory. Making the point dramatically, Sherman ordered Savannah's slave auction blocks cut up and distributed for firewood.

Since peace on earth did not exist in Georgia for Fanny Cohen, she also foreswore good will. She called in several friends and relatives for a "*rebel* meeting. . . . We abused the Yankees to our hearts content." A guest told them of a new paper with a Northern bias, the *Savannah Daily Loyal Georgian,* emblazoned with the slogan, "Redeemed, regenerated, and disenthralled—the Union, It Must and Shall be preserved." (In the hostile local climate it would publish only three issues.) Since the Rebel visitors were certain that their South would rise again, the maxim "of course created great merriment, the first time I had a hearty laugh since the Goths had been among us." Sherman's orders were that only two newspapers could be published daily. Both would be former Confederate organs, but, he wrote, "their editors and proprietors would be held to the strictest accountability, and will be punished severely, in person and property, for a libelous publication, mischievous matter, premature news, unsupported statements, or any comments whatever upon the acts of constituted authorities. . . ." Rancor would be confined to such salons as that of Fanny and her friends.

The Christmas spirit also failed the fostering efforts of Captain Charles Belknap. He had brought to Savannah the abandoned little girls he and other Federals had found near Sandersville, and asked city authorities to try to find a home for them. No one appeared interested in "the little white trash." A wounded young lieutenant who was being shipped home to recuperate volunteered to take them north, where they found, Belknap later wrote, "happy homes."

IN THE RAIN through Christmas Day, troops were mustered briefly in unit strength to listen to their sergeants read the general's proud message of congratulations for "so complete a success . . . that it entitles it to a place in the military history of the world." On dismissal, although interrupted by outbreaks of heavy rain, troops began to cook their Christmas dinners. Few were lodged in the city. Even their officers remained with the men, appropriating the best sites for shelter and drainage in the environs of the damp old city. "We dug a hole in the sandy ground, 6½ feet long, 3½ feet wide, 4 ft deep," Private Upson wrote about his spot, shared with Possum, his buddy during the march, "and lined it with boards we got out of an old house, put our tent over it, got a lot of hanging [Spanish] moss off a tree, put it in the bottom and have a very comfortable place to sleep. We do not have much duty to do and can go around a good deal."

"Going around" largely meant scrounging for food. Provisions remained short. Supply ships steaming up that were not shallow-draft vessels had to be unloaded from lighters because of uncleared harbor blockage. (An officer from the Inspector General's Department would later charge, obtusely, "inexcusable delay in furnishing rations to the army. . . . The QM & Commissary Depts failed most signally to supply this command with necessary subsistence.")

The headquarters mess of the 16th Illinois had a Christmas feast that included rice and goose but largely consisted of oysters—fried and roasted, boiled in soup, and raw on the half shell. "A little top-heavy as to oysters," said Colonel Charles Kerr, "but we don't complain." Major William Humphrey of the 101st Illinois did complain, writing his family, "While you were all eating your good dinner we soldiers would have been glad to have the crumbs that fell from your table. I will tell you what our meals were this day: Breakfast, rice and beef. Dinner, rice. Supper, beef and rice. Rice is our favorite dish now." Private Frederick Buerstatte recorded a dinner of "crackers, rice and meat." Sergeant Rice Bull wrote later* of a "lean and hungry Christmas. . . . While the Armies nearer home in Virginia and Tennessee were having their turkey dinners, furnished and forwarded to them by the people of the North, we at Savannah, were so far away we could not be reached. We had boiled rice, Georgia beef that was left from those driven along with us on our march through the state, and coffee." James Sawyer, an unschooled private with a similar Christmas dinner, wrote home with an idealism that was not widely shared, "I can afoard to go hungry somb times if it will help free the slaves."

In Andersonville Prison, Private Stearns reported Christmas Eve dinner as "meal, sweet potatoes & salt," and Christmas Day rations as, again, "meal, sweet potatoes & salt. I thought of home and the loved ones there and it made me sad to think that I was not among them."

In Savannah for the day on a pass, John Peters found a shop selling tobacco and watched "a lot of Officers running horse Races." The word

---

* At seventy-one in 1913, on retiring from the Mutual National Bank in Troy, New York, and the Troy and New England Railroad, for which he was secretary-treasurer, Rice C. Bull returned to his wartime diary and expanded it into a memoir.

spread. Soldiers flocked to Savannah's abandoned racetrack, where spirited horses abducted from plantations along the march were jockeyed and noisy betting flourished. The raucous Christmas jollity got out of hand. When Sherman learned of it, he issued a ban. Another scrape involved whiskey, although the provost marshal's men continued to keep troops out of liquor shops. As Sergeant Olney Andrus of the 95th Illinois wrote home, "Col. Tom turned out 15 galls of Rotgut & several of the boys got Happy, and some got pugilistic, and as a consequence some had Eyes Red & some Black. . . ."*

IT WAS A VERY DIFFERENT CHRISTMAS for the Confederate troops that had evacuated Savannah. The 165 horsemen of Colonel Joseph H. Lewis's 9th Kentucky "Orphan Brigade" had been called into Savannah on December 15. After hanging on the flank of the march to disrupt the advance any way they could, the mounted Kentuckians were useless in the city and ordered into South Carolina. They marked their holiday in chilly Hardeeville. The year before, in a drizzling rain, they had celebrated Christmas Eve in Dalton, just across the Georgia border from Chattanooga, with "pine top" whiskey distilled from the tips of pine boughs. Some became so tipsy that they vigorously sang "The Star-Spangled Banner" before being silenced. The next day their Christmas dinner was bean soup. A Kentuckian wrote in his company's clothing account book, "*Another* Christmas has come and gone, and we are still combatting with the Vandal horde; are likely to be doing that same thing next Christmas. What a pity."

At that next Christmas, in Hardeeville, from which they would have

---

* Col. Thomas W. Humphrey of the 95th Illinois had been killed in action June 10, 1864. Sgt. Andrus apparently did not know the name of his current regimental commander (Col. Leander Blanden)—or was still under the influence of the Christmas moonshine.

to retreat further, cavalryman Johnny Green wrote, "Peace on Earth, Good will to men should prevail. We certainly would preserve the peace if they would go home & let us alone." As a holiday treat the men were issued soap and bathed in the cold Savannah River. Christmas dinner for the Kentuckians was rice and small portions of sweet potatoes and pork. It rained all evening.

Christmas Day along the routes impacted by Sherman's march was bleak almost everywhere. Former Atlantans had begun returning to their shattered city, finding shelter in the homes of more fortunate friends or in temporary shacks built by local entrepreneurs. Not all of the devastation had been by the Federals. Filling the vacuum as they left were myriad thieves, Rebel deserters, bushwhackers, and even opportunistic townspeople axed Atlanta's trees for fuel and stripped anything salvageable from abandoned properties, even bricks and boards.

Only Atlanta's First Baptist Church, where the Rev. Henry C. Hornaday delivered the sermon, reopened for Christmas. At Thomas Maguire's Promised Land Plantation near Stone Mountain, where the main house built in 1820 had escaped burning, Maguire, who had whipped three slaves for alleged stealing several days before, and expected to keep his slaves docile and indefinitely, noted indulgently about his family's holiday, "Not much fuss this morning by the little ones about Christmas. Not like it used to be. . . ."

In Covington, at the Burge plantation passed early in the march and ransacked by bummers, Dolly Burge had noted in her diary on Christmas Eve, "We are all Sad. . . . I have nothing to put even in Sadai[']s stocking which hangs so invitingly for Santa Claus . . . though I have explained to her why he could not come." On Christmas, "Sadai jumped out of bed very early this morning to feel in her stocking. She could not believe but she would find something in it. She crept back into bed[,] pulled the covers over her face & I soon heard her sobbing. The little negroes all came in [appealing,] 'Christmas gift mistress Christmas gift mistress.' I pulled the cover over my face & was soon mingling my tears with Sadai[']s."

At her plantation, Montivideo, south of Savannah, Mary Jones had found "five Yankees" revisiting on Christmas Eve, after she had assumed that ransacking was over. She and a local friend, Kate King, "went down as usual, with beating hearts and knees that smote together, yet trusting in our God for protection." The soldiers—almost certainly bummers— claimed that they were searching for arms. Mrs. Jones explained that "even the minutest drawer or trunk" had already been examined, and that their officers had said that troops could not enter private dwellings. No officer was with them, they said. "We are independent scouts and do as we please." One, described as a "Dutchman," explained that they were not after money. "If you have two or three thousand dollars, I would not touch it." Confederate dollars were practically useless. But he warned, "The house will make a beautiful fire and a great smoke." The bummers poked about from the attic to the cellar and left, taking nothing but a sewing bag emptied of spools.

THE WOMEN ASSUMED the worst about Savannah, and learned soon in a note brought to them from a neighbor by Cato, one of the plantation's slaves, that the city had been evacuated, the Yankees capturing thirty thousand bales of cotton and "nine hundred prisoners"—the abandoned sick and wounded. Frightened, the women, with five children, spent the night before Christmas huddled "upstairs in one room with closed windows and a dim light."

On their very bleak Christmas Day, Mrs. Jones's daughter Mary Mallard observed "two Yankees riding around the lot, but seeing nothing to take away; and we were not further interrupted." Still, two Montivideo slaves, George and June, reported that their oxcart "had been cut

SAVANNAH UNDER THE UNION FLAG

to pieces and the oxen killed." They had gone as far as the Ogeechee, "where George saw Mr. Mallard, & says he preached to the Yankees."* The younger Mary's husband, the Rev. Robert Quarterman Mallard, pastor of the Central Presbyterian Church in Atlanta until the siege, and a chaplain in the local Home Guard since, had been seized. "They had put no handcuffs on him, and he was walking at large, and they gave him plenty to eat."

Under Geary's discipline, Savannah fared better than the outlying

---

* Mallard preached to both his captors and his fellow prisoners of war.

plantations. After Christmas services a local church sponsored a special food collection for the city orphan asylum. Both Union troops and residents contributed freely, prompting a soldier observing the scene to remark, "It did not seem as though we were enemies." Elsewhere in the area, a Federal captain and ninety men loaded wagons with provisions from their improving stocks onto wagons for the needy and carted them below Savannah to a poor area that both Confederate and Union troops had stripped bare. As a further gesture to the season, soldiers tied twigs to the heads of the mules, converting them to reindeer.

NINE

Christmas Week in the Union

U NTIL THE MARCH RESUMED, GENERAL GEARY remained Sherman's military governor of the Savannah area, now restored to the Union. "I am now the *Commandante* of the City," he boasted to his wife, "in honor of its capture by me, and of the surrender to me." Yet he had not fought his way into Savannah, and was in charge largely because of his peacetime experience as mayor of raw San Francisco. "He very soon established a good police, maintained admirable order," Sherman wrote, "and I doubt if Savannah, either before or since, has had a better government than during our stay. The guard-mountings and parades, as well as the greater reviews, became the daily resorts of the ladies, to hear the music of our excellent bands; schools were reopened, and the churches every Sunday were well filled with the most respectful congregations; stores were reopened, and markets for provisions, meat, and wood, were established, so that each family, regardless of race, color, or opinion, could procure all the necessaries and even luxuries of life, provided they had money. Of course many families were destitute of this, and to these were issued stores from our own stock of supplies."

Sherman's recollection was not quite the immediate reality. As the churches on Christmas Day evidenced, the people of Savannah—the remaining adult population was largely female—were sullen, and while the clergy preached submission to the facts, and saddened parishioners brushed away tears, some were less resigned. Several ladies, according to a reporter with the occupation, called upon the provost marshal, Major General Frank Blair, a handlebar-mustached Missourian who before the war had owned slaves, "and unfolded a horrible story of suffering and woe." Blair was moved and sat down to write orders for what was referred to by the command as "gratuitous distribution," expressing his hope that the war, with its privations, would soon be over. "This war won't be terminated," one of the supplicants snapped, turning his remark back at him, "until you kill all the men, and then we women will fight you, and if you kill all of us, it won't be ended then, for we'll come back as ghosts to haunt you."

The general quietly shredded the commissary order. "If such be the case," he said, "I think you might as well die of starvation, as then your ghosts may be too weak to come back and haunt us." And he "coolly but politely bowed the discomfited lady mendicants into the street."

When tempers eased, the women were supplied, but about two hundred residents, mostly families of men in the Confederate service, preferred to exit the occupation and follow the fortunes of their husbands and fathers. Escorted by Sherman's aide Captain John C. Audenreid, they were sent in a steamboat under a flag of truce to Charleston.

Sherman's rules for Savannah were laid down in detail in his Special Field Order No. 141 the day after Christmas. Under military authority, the mayor and council would continue to exercise such functions as keeping streets "cleaned and lighted" and fire companies functioning, and assembling "the names and number of worthy families that need assistance and support." The city fathers would encourage residents "to resume their usual pursuits." Since the army was to disturb families "as little as possible in their residences, and tradesmen allowed the free use of their shops, tools, etc.," troops in the city as a local constabulary began constructing, with the aid of freed blacks, temporary shelters in public parks. "All our squares," Fanny Cohen complained disparagingly after a carriage ride on the twenty-seventh, "[are] built up with wooden houses so that I scarcely recognized the streets."*

The day before, she wrote, a "Yankee" had visited Octavus Cohen, "and although I did no more than bow when he entered he had the impertinence to ask me to play the piano for him. I, of course, declined the honor and the evening's conversation. If we are conquered I see no reason why we should receive our enemies as our friends and I shall never do it as long as I live. Father is very much afraid that I will compromise him by my too open avowal of hatred, but I pray daily that he may be mistaken in his fears." She was pleased to discover that even her Aunt Belle, a former Philadelphian, remained "violent against the Yankees and a true sympathizer in our cause." Fanny's compatriot Frances Howard was pleased at the report that when her sister and a Miss Moodie visited Charles Green to inquire about some confiscated cotton and were asked if they would like to be introduced to his guest, General Sherman, Miss Moodie protested, "Not for the world! I have no wish to make his acquaintance; my business is private and entirely with you." As she and Nelly Howard passed the general's "beautifully furnished rooms" with an air of disgust, Green asked, "Don't you want him to rest comfortably?"

"Indeed not," Nelly claimed she said. "I wish a thousand papers of

---

* Under the limited force left after Sherman, the shoddy shacks would deteriorate badly.

pins were stuck in that bed and that he was strapped down to them." She also alleged Federal excesses, almost certainly at second hand and some perhaps imaginative. "Our cemetery is desecrated with their fortifications. The Yankees have broken open the doors and vaults, and in one instance that I know of, the coffin of a lady was opened and a cross and chain stolen from her body. Surely such men are not human."

An unsubmissive elderly woman passing General Howard's headquarters stepped into the sandy street to avoid a Union flag overhanging the sidewalk. "Walk under the flag, Madam," a sentry at the door said. When she refused, he took her indoors before Oliver Howard.

"Madam," said the general, "I understand that you refused to pass under my flag."

"I did. Am I not at liberty to walk in the sand if I prefer it to the sidewalk?"

"Yes, but you intentionally avoided my flag." Almost certainly unseriously he added, "I'll make you walk under it."

"You cannot make me. You may have me carried under it, but it will be your act, not mine."

Playing along with her intransigence, the gentlemanly Howard threatened, "I'll have you sent to prison."

"Send me if you will. I know you have the power. See if you can shake my resolution."

"I'll have the flag hung in front of your door, so you can't go out without walking under it."

"Then I'll stay at home and send the servants. They won't mind."

Amused, Howard sent her on her way.

Most Savannah women, the correspondent for the *Cincinnati Commercial* observed, went about in a mood of dejection rather than defiance. After years of war and blockade, the ladies, aside from their well-worn Christmas Day finery, "have gone far back into discarded wardrobes for their walking habits. They affect black, mostly. They wear hats with faded ribbons, or bonnets of antiquated design. They do not pile up their own hair and everybody else's they can lay hands on. . . . There is something touching in the plainness of their dress, suggestive here and there of having been turned, and worked over, with whatever touch of coquetry their reduced circumstances, or perhaps opportunities, would permit." Recognizing the inevitable, Fanny Cohen went to her bedroom one day during Christmas week, "and darned my stockings." Her maid had been sick, and, once recovered, could opt for freedom whenever she wanted to chance the break. It was "the first time I had ever done such a thing in my life. But I suppose when she leaves me, I shall always have to do so. I had better begin at once."

In a city long without its familiar young men, some Savannah ladies smiled, and even waved, from their porches and balconies. A few were even more friendly. Major George Ward Nichols wrote of seeing soldiers "lounging on the doorsteps of the houses in cheerful conversation with fair damsels." According to Colonel Oscar Jackson, "The ladies are the tastiest 'Secesh' I have seen, and I rather think [they] would get to like Yankees. The majority do not look a bit mad now." Writing to his sister in Illinois, Captain Charles Wills confided, "I found the sweetest girl here that ever man looked at . . . , with large very deep brown eyes, almost black that sparkle like Stars. I swear I was never so bewitched before." Fifty years later, when she edited her brother's letters for publication, she deleted the lines.

Restaurants, saloons and theaters reopened, as well as dance halls where the partners that soldiers paid for were black. Despite a nine o'clock curfew requiring that men had to be back in camp, bordellos flourished and were so numerous that a private, Samuel Jarrett, complained about the frequency of standing duty outside them to inhibit unruliness, "There are so many hore houses in town which must have a Sentinel at each door for to keep them Straight." The 58th Indiana's slapped-together shanties and buttoned-together tents stood within an increasingly garbage-strewn enclosure behind a whorehouse. "It is rather a vile place," Chaplain John Hight wrote, "to come a thousand miles to camp."

Official restrictions for residents were not onerous. No person was to pass an outer picket line without written permission. "Commerce with the outer world" would be "governed by the restrictions and rules of the Treasury Department." The use of Confederate money was not forbidden, but merchants accepted it at their risk, and a Northern bank would soon open to deal only in Union dollars. Residents needed wages in Union currency, and by Sherman's edict the army was to furnish where possible "suitable employment to the people, white and black, or transport them to such points as they may choose where employment can be had." Laborers were recruited to refit buildings for the use of the army, for shops to be put at the service of a Treasury agent for trade, and for parapets to defend the city from possible Rebel attacks. When a black regiment, the 110th Colored Troops, arrived in Savannah, Sherman had the men disarmed and employed as laborers, teamsters, and servants, subverting the War Department's intentions to use blacks as ordinary soldiers. He declared it "wise, so far to respect the prejudices of the people of Savannah, not to garrison the place with negro troops. It seems a perfect buggery to them, and I know that all people are more influenced by prejudice than by reason."

One resident who began helping herself, Sherman recalled, was a lady he had known before the rebellion, Josephine Goodwin, who told him that "with a barrel of flour and some sugar" which she had received gratuitously from the commissary, she had baked cakes and pies, in the sale of which she realized a profit of fifty-six Union dollars. With cheap, almost worthless, Rebel money, games of chuck-a-luck, dice, and poker proliferated in encampments and even along the slopes of railway embankments. After losing all his money on the twenty-sixth, Private Peters pawned his watch the next day for twenty dollars and went back to poker.

On the twenty-ninth he picked up another pass and went into town for billiards. It was a good war.

CONCEDING THE FALL OF SAVANNAH, the *Richmond Enquirer* registered Confederate frustration with Sherman's conciliatory policies in the city, failing to realize that even while Hardee prepared his last-ditch defenses, townspeople went to bed nightly in fear that their slaves would rise. It did not happen because blacks knew that Sherman was coming, and they did not need to risk their deliverance. With a benign occupation, residents, however despondent about the future of the rebellion, were safe, and even becoming comfortable. "We demand public meetings in Georgia," the organ of the Confederacy expostulated emptily. "We want to hear the voices of our brave and true patriots, to rally the men, comfort the feeble, and warn those who confide in the transparent cheat of the Yankees." In Richmond, too, war office clerk John Jones on December 27 conceded "fog and gloom" in the Confederate capital on press confirmation of the catastrophe, rumored since Christmas Eve. "Men are silent, and some dejected. It is unquestionably the darkest period we have yet experienced." The day before, although the news remained unconfirmed, he had written in his diary, "The Georgians in Lee's army are more or less demoralized, and a reward of a sixty days' furlough is given for shooting any deserter from our ranks."

AS THE HARBOR WAS BEING CLEARED of obstructions, a blockade runner slipped in by night and anchored, assuming that Savannah remained a Rebel stronghold. At first light, panic struck among the crew, but the *Rebecca Hertz* had nowhere to go. Federals relieved it of its sugar, coffee, and tea. Legitimate traffic began docking daily with mail and provisions, and another letter from Grant, dated December 27, was en route, rescinding any plans for moving the army to Virginia by sea. Sherman realized that the idea was unworkable. Winter storms lingering about Cape Hatteras foreclosed the mass transport of troops, but he had gone along. He would be authorized to march through the Carolinas, threatening the Confederate interior until he linked up with Grant or pinched Lee's forces into surrender.

Winter storms had also ravaged the middle South during Christmas week, where Sherman after Atlanta had sent surplus divisions to General Thomas in Tennessee. While the snows melted below Nashville, John Hood's demoralized army struggled to retreat on dirt roads that had become bogs, but the weather also hampered pursuit. Increasingly melancholy after Christmas whiskey, Captain Samuel T. Foster of a Texas brigade wrote in his diary, "This is Christmas 1864. Where were we last Christmas, or two years ago? If we had counted noses then, and again today, the missing would outnumber the present." The last of the Confederates would escape over the Tennessee River in northern Alabama from Christmas night under torchlight through December 28, on a makeshift bridge made possible by fifteen pontoon boats abandoned earlier by the Federals, which had floated opportunely toward the Johnnies. As the strong current twisted the span, troops walked across cautiously in single file.

In Savannah, Sherman began to plan his "Project for January." He also responded without enthusiasm to the suggestion that he be promoted to lieutenant general, a rank held only by the general-in-chief. "I will accept no commission," he wrote, that would tend to create a rivalry with Grant. "I want him to hold what he has earned and got. I have all the rank I want. I would rather be engineer of a railroad, than President of the United States. I have commanded a hundred thousand men in battle, and on the march, successfully and without confusion, and that is enough for reputation. Now, I want rest and peace, and they are only to be had through war." When Grant saw the text he sent a copy to his wife, Julia, writing that "Sherman's letter shows how noble a man he is. How few there are who when rising to popular favor as he now is would stop to say [such] a word. . . ."

From a newspaper arriving in Savannah by sea, the *New York Herald* of December 22, Sherman learned of the death, from pneumonia, of his six-month-old son, Charles, on December 4. It was his second loss of a child. He had never seen the boy. Sherman found, he wrote to Ellen, "a full obituary and notice of funeral ceremonies. . . . I cannot say that I grieve for him as I did [for] Willy, for he was but a mere ideal, whereas Willy was incorporated with us. . . . But amid the Scenes of death and desolation through which I daily pass I cannot but become callous to death. . . . You on the Contrary surrounded alone by life & youth cannot take things so philosophically but are stayed by the Religious faith[*] of a better and higher life elsewhere[.] I should like to have seen the baby of which all spoke so well, but I seem destined to pass my life away so that even my children will be strangers."

Christmas and an interim of peace inevitably led to thoughts of home among Sherman's troops, who put their longings into letters that could now be posted to loved ones. Few other than the badly wounded and returned prisoners were actually going back, but Oliver Howard, who had a brood of young children, asked for leave sufficient to spend "two days at home."

"Howard," said Sherman, "I'd give a million dollars, if I had it, to be with my children. Would you do more than that?"

"I'll say no more," Howard conceded.

---

[*] Ellen, a Roman Catholic, had moved during wartime from Lancaster, Ohio, to South Bend, Indiana, to have her children educated at Catholic schools there. The elaborate burial rites were at the Church of the Sacred Heart at Notre Dame.

* * *

CHRISTMAS WEEK IN THE SOUTH was dreary at best. On the twenty-seventh, Mary Chesnut traveled from Columbia to Camden. South Carolina, she realized, was surely Sherman's next target. "The very dismalest Christmas overtook us there," she wrote. "Foreign bat[talion]s in full fig saw us on the train. Miss Rhett went with us. A brilliant woman—and very agreeable. Which brilliant are not always. She said: 'The world, you know, is composed of men, women—and Rhetts.* Now, we feel that if we are to lose our negroes, we would as soon see Sherman free them as the Confederate government. Freeing negroes seems the last Confederate government craze.'" Mrs. Chesnut felt that the South was "a little bit too slow about it." She appended a poem to her diary, beginning, "Darkest of all Decembers. . . ."

In Charleston the same day, irreconcilable author William Gilmore Simms deplored to his son the "criminality and stupidity" of the Jefferson Davis regime, which had "brought the war to our doors." He had written an anti-abolitionist novel, *The Sword and the Distaff*, in response to *Uncle Tom's Cabin*, which he considered unfair, and although he considered himself a mild, patriarchal, master, the slaves on his plantation were immediately at risk. So, too, with the approach of Federal troops, would be everything else he owned.

In Walthourville, Mary Jones Mallard recorded the twenty-seventh with "No enemy today. Bless the Lord for this mercy!" The next day

---

* Her contrarian brothers, Trescot and Robert Rhett, Jr., members of the South Carolina legislature, opposed Jefferson Davis's desperate proposal in November that the Confederacy purchase from their owners 40,000 slaves for noncombatant service, after which they would be freed. Also, that if white soldiers could not guarantee Southern independence, slaves be sent into combat with them. The Rhetts called the startling proposals unconstitutional interference with the states' rights to control slavery.

was equally quiet. But on the following afternoon "three Yankees and one Negro" broke open the door, although her mother reminded the bummers of General Sherman's orders to leave civilians alone. Two loyal slaves pretended to be disabled, and another warned the intruders successfully about stealing, describing their haul as "Them dead people clothes!" Then it was quiet into the new year.

On New Year's Eve, Joseph LeConte was still trying to reach his Georgia plantation, Syphax, in Liberty County, traveling a roundabout 850 miles southwest from South Carolina rather than chance the 45 miles across the Savannah from Hardeeville to Union-occupied Walthourville. As an officer disguised in civilian garb, however scruffy and travel tattered, he would be in serious trouble if taken prisoner. LeConte was resigned to the loss of his slaves and land. Yet it still seemed, he wrote in his diary, "a wickedness, a sacrilege . . . to doubt for a single moment the final success of *our Cause*." He found everyone in despair. "The Georgia militia, taken from their homes and farms and unaccustomed to camp life, are in favor of peace on any terms. News of the fall of Savannah received this week renders the gloom still deeper." He had reached a town "full of refugees from Liberty and from Savannah" and saw nothing but calamity in the Confederate future. "Sons, brothers, husbands, fathers have been freely sacrificed; for this[,] earnest agonizing prayers have gone up from every church and every family circle. O God! And must it fail at last!"[†]

---

†   In 1869, through the good offices of Louis Agassiz at Harvard, and Brigadier General Barton S. Alexander, a Union engineer in charge of coastal fortifications at San Francisco harbor, Joseph LeConte and his brother, John, left South Carolina to become professors at the new University of California, to be located in Berkeley. Joseph would be professor of chemistry and acting president, its first chief executive, and, in the 1870s, John, professor of physics, would become president. In the last months of the war Joseph LeConte was in hiding, as he had been in charge, as a chemist, of Confederate explosives manufacturing and procurement.

* * *

Every day after Christmas in Savannah, even in intermittent cold rain, regimental bands paraded down sandy, once-graceful Bull Street, its paving stones gone at General Hardee's order to blockade the harbor. For reasons of discipline, Sherman wanted to give his troops something to do. The small daughters of a Confederate cavalry officer, Nelly and Daisy Gordon watched the passing troops, asking, "Oh, Mama, is that Sherman?" Eleanor Gordon confessed that she could not identify him: "I never saw old Sherman." When the band of the 2nd Wisconsin marched by, Daisy protested, "Just hear them playing 'When This Cruel War Is Over' and they're doing it theirselves all this time!" Many songs had been appropriated by both sides, with much different lyrics. First published in Brooklyn, the sentimental ballad was republished in Savannah with new lines about "God and Freedom," and "our Southern Banner— Emblem of the Free." (Some songs that Southerners found especially insolent could not be lyrically reversed—as with the oft-played "John Brown's Body.")

When the 10th Michigan paraded with XIV Corps on the clear and sunny twenty-seventh, brass buttons and gun barrels gleaming, Corydon Foote's much-polished silver mountings on his snare drum gleamed as he marched, sticks flying, one pace behind the regimental color bearer. He knew it would be his last duty. His three-year enlistment—in 1862 he had been one of 127 thirteen-year-olds in the Union Army—was up on January 12, and he was too old now to remain a drummer while too young and too small for the infantry. Uncle Billy sat atop Sam as the regiments passed in review. Sherman wore his dress uniform as a major general, with his two stars and gold braid and the lone white shirt he had packed for the campaign. Most troops had never seen him so splendidly attired.

* * *

SHERMAN DID MATERIALIZE at Eleanor Gordon's home during Christmas week, with letters from her father, Union colonel John H. Kinzie of Chicago, an old friend. Eleanor's husband, William Gordon, a captain in Wheeler's cavalry, would be embittered by Sherman's visit, writing to her in unyielding terms a message he slipped through to Savannah, "The fact of your being in the Federal lines is of course difficult to bear, but I accept that as the fate of war and will endure it as I would any sacrifice that may be called for. But what really galls me is that you should associate with my enemies upon any terms than those politeness demands from every lady."

When Sherman visited, the girls had darted timidly behind their mother. Drawing Nelly forward, Mrs. Gordon said, "General, here is a little girl who was very anxious to see 'old Sherman' the day of the parade." Nelly denied saying "old Sherman," claiming that it was Daisy (Juliette), who also pleaded innocence. The general, missing his own children, took the girls up on his knees. "Why of course you never said 'old Sherman,' because you and I used to play together when I was a little boy, and now we're going to sit right down and talk it over."

They laughed at the absurdity, and chatted until it was well past bedtime for the girls, after which Sherman offered Eleanor Gordon his much-cleansed reminiscences of the march from Atlanta.

Another visitor who also knew Eleanor's father was Oliver Howard, who, one-handed, nestled the girls close to him. He missed his own five daughters. "Oh, you have only got one arm!" exclaimed Daisy.

"Yes, little girl. Aren't you sorry for me?"

"Yes, indeed. What happened to your arm?"

"It was shot off in battle."

"Oh, did the Yankees shoot it off?"

"No, my dear. The Rebels shot it off."

"Did they?" said Daisy. "Well, I shouldn't wonder if my papa did it. He's shot lots of Yankees."

Innocently, Daisy was as well indoctrinated as her mother was compliant. Heeding her husband's instructions, the docile Eleanor Gordon and her children left the safety of Savannah and sailed under a flag of truce to Charleston.*

ON THE TWENTY-EIGHTH, Mayor Richard Arnold convened a meeting at the request of the remaining aldermen of Savannah. "When the city was taken," he told the assembly, ". . . you asked protection. You all know that it was granted to you, and we all feel deeply indebted to Brig. Gen. Geary for his conduct as commandant of the city." He then asked citizens to appoint a chairman to guide them in formulating any resolutions they wished to propose to the occupation authorities. Some were formalities, but the third promised obedience to United States law in exchange for continued protection "over our persons, lives, and property recognized by those laws." (In effect that recognized the end of slavery in Savannah.) The fourth asked that the governor of Georgia call a constitutional convention over the issue of continuing the war. The fifth asked Sherman to continue the administration of Savannah under John Geary, "who has by his urbanity as a gentleman and his uniform kindness to our citizens, done all in his power to protect them and their property from insult and injury," and they unanimously offered thanks to him and the officers under his command.

On the same day, Sherman reviewed Frank Blair's XVII Corps, which

---

* They returned after the war. William W. Gordon would found the city's new cotton exchange. Juliette, who would marry William Low of Savannah, became founder of the Girl Scouts of America.

FEDERALS MARCHING THROUGH SAVANNAH

marched with regimental bands playing "Rally Round the Flag." (By the first parade, troops had received new issues of shoes, discarding footwear often held together with strips of cloth or string.) Each day in the waning week, a parade, with martial music, roused soldiers from soggy fields and tents. Porches, windows, and even housetops along Bay Street were crowded, but local curiosity, according to the correspondent for the *Philadelphia Inquirer*, was probably much disappointed by the orderly, beflagged march. "They had, no doubt, expected to see each man carrying his bundle of plunder, with perhaps an infant perched upon his bayonet and a negro at his heels."

The major event on December 30 was the queuing up at the provost marshal's office, in the Exchange Building, of male citizens claiming unwilling former service to the Confederate cause and now availing themselves of President Lincoln's amnesty proclamation of December 8, 1863. With a signature, each resumed fealty to the national flag and (but for goods relating to treason and rebellion) received "a restoration of all rights of property except as to slaves." Conspicuously absent in the queue, and very likely not in Savannah at all, were former (and ineligible) officers or agents of the rejected Union who had aided the rebellion.

It was already an American tradition, North and South, that festive parades be punctuated by a procession of local firefighting equipage. In the mid-1850s, 487 slaves and 140 free blacks comprised the Savannah Fire Department, supplemented by white volunteer companies. The blacks paraded annually, singing loudly "as the sound of many waters," according to an observer, on the last Friday in May, reviewed by the mayor and alderman. By Sherman's order, Christmas week revived the suspended tradition. The culminating "reviewing carnival" came on New Year's Eve. The *Inquirer*, in a dispatch dated December 31, reported that the gaudy march:

> came off today. The city fire companies—all colored— according to previous arrangements, had the honor of doing the display for the last day of the year. After parading the streets for some time they were reviewed in due order by Generals Sherman and Geary. It is impossible to do this affair justice, . . . a whole Broadway full of immaculate blacks, in dress less uniform than Jacob's cattle,* and ranging in size from the six-footer to the merest piccaninny, . . . all marching through the city and chanting some unearthly song, not

---

* Genesis 32: "all the speckled and spotted cattle, and all the brown cattle."

a word of which is intelligible to the uninitiated. . . . Their officers are distinguished by fantastic hats and coats, which were gotten up by sole reference to many colors. . . .

The [fire] engines are of the oldest pattern, and their hook and ladder is the invention which proved such a failure at the conflagration of Sodom and Gomorrah. . . .

It was only when they stopped to cheer our officers that the music (?) ceased.

As the shops selling liquor had been guarded by provost marshals since troops entered Savannah, there was relatively little drunkenness from Christmas into the new year. Henry Hitchcock noted the arrests of two intoxicated and unruly soldiers, and even the Confederate *Augusta Chronicle* picked up the story, reporting, to Federal credit, strangely, "The most perfect order is maintained in the city. No soldier is allowed to interfere with the citizens in any particular. A citizen was arrested by a drunken soldier a few days since"—it was Christmas week—"who knocked the soldier down. The officer of the guard said nothing to the citizen, but had the soldier taken to the barracks, gagged and soundly whipped for his misbehavior. A drunken soldier who undertook to create a disturbance recently, and refused to allow himself to be arrested, was shot down by the guard at once."

New Year's Eve was another local exception. Private Peters confessed that his squad of the 10th Illinois "got on a hell of a drunk." William Lloyd of a New Jersey regiment confessed to his wife in a misspelled letter, "Last night I had plenty of Whiskey but to day I have none, we had canteens full and we had a merry old Time. They broke all my furniture, tore my table cloth, and tore evry thing upside down, I thought I would fire a saulute, I got my musket and fired it, and I set my tent a fire, and by the time I got through, my tent was most burnt up. New Years don't come but once a year, & tents are cheap." So, apparently, was local moonshine.

BEFORE SUCH INCIDENTAL EXCEPTIONS to discipline, Sherman had written to his father-in-law, Thomas Ewing, of his satisfaction with the army's "experience and adhesion." That quality, he felt, had kept under control the "disorganizing tendency" that foraging encouraged. "I have just reviewed my *four* Corps and challenge competition for soldierly bearing & behavior. No City was ever occupied with less disorder or more system than this of Savannah, and it is a subject of universal"—he meant widespread—"comment that though an army of 60,000 men lay camped around it, women & children of an Hostile People walk its streets with as much security as they do in Philadelphia."

Although Sherman was employing black labor, civilian and soldier, to reinforce the redoubts about Savannah so that the city could be secured with a small establishment when he continued his march into South Carolina and beyond, he had to figure out what to do with liberated slaves who, however unauthorized, might otherwise follow him further north. Visiting early in the new year, Secretary of War Stanton suggested providing small farm plots, and a Freedmen's Bureau to be set up in Washington. Deflecting any notion that black soldiers, some already sent to him, might guard Savannah to free his veteran units for further operations, Sherman wrote to Grant on the last day of the year that "white troops would be best as the People are dreadfully alarmed lest we garrison the place with Negros. Now no matter what the negro soldiers are[,] you Know that people have prejudices which must be regarded. Prejudice like Religion cannot be discussed."

To his brother, Senator John Sherman, he wrote with satisfaction of receiving "vast numbers of letters from distinguished men, awarding me a measure of praise higher than the case calls for, but looking back I surely have done my full share in this war, and would like to slide out quietly and See more of my family. . . . As it is I must go on. Such success has attended me that every officer & man with me thinks he would be lost unless I am at hand. I hear the Soldiers talk as I ride by—There goes the old man. All's Right—not a waver, doubt or hesitation when I order, and men march to certain death without a murmur if I call on them because they Know I value their lives as much as my own." To Ellen as the year closed he wrote sadly of having never seen his infant son, but also proudly about concluding "a Campaign which Judges pronounce will be famous among the Grand deeds of the world. I can hardly realize it for really it was easy, but like one who has walked a narrow plank I look back and wonder if I really did it; but here I am in the proud City of Savannah. . . ." People, he knew, talked about the war drawing to a close, but he did not yet have their certitude. "There remains yet a large class of Southern men who will not have Peace, and They still have the power to do much mischief."

Remote from that class, a relieved Savannah resident wrote to his brother in Rochester, New York, on the last day of the year that he felt "delivered from an Egyptian bondage." Originally from England, he had been compelled, nevertheless, to "join the Confederate service" and had been in the Rebel navy. There was little to buy and no Union dollars to buy it, he wrote, as bread was two dollars a pound and salt a dollar. An eight-pound sack of flour went for $150 and eggs were sixteen dollars a dozen. (General Geary would soon regulate the prices of all articles of common use, limiting butter to twenty-five cents a pound, cheese to fifty cents, preserved meats to a dollar per tin, a chicken to a dollar-fifty.) "I would take advantage of a free passage, now—which is granted to all in the Confederate service who take the [Union] oath—but I don't think I could endure a northern winter, after living so long in this warm country."

Uncowed, Frances Howard could not endure the new dispensation.

Nevertheless, she had nowhere else to go and nowhere to be prudently rebellious but in her own tightly curtained town house, where she wrote in her diary despondently about the last day of 1864, "The city authorities have seen fit to declare the city once more in the Union." For Savannah the war was over.

AFTERWORD

The final verse of "Marching through Georgia" summed up the two-pronged thrust from Atlanta to the sea with deadly accuracy:

> *So we made a thoroughfare for freedom*
>   *and her train,*
> *Sixty miles of latitude, three hundred to the main;*
> *Treason fled before us, for resistance was in vain*
> *While we were marching through Georgia.*

The week of Savannah was the final Christmas of the War between the States, in terms of casualties the costliest conflict ever fought in America, or by Americans.

The war's first Christmas occurred before a shot was fired, five days after a secessionist convention in South Carolina in December 1860 declared that the state was no longer a part of the Union, putting at risk Fort Sumter in Charleston harbor. On Christmas Day 1861, Lincoln's Cabinet met in Washington to discuss the dilemma arising from the capture of Confederate envoys James Mason and John Slidell from a British mail packet at sea, which an outraged government in London, openly pro-South in any case, viewed as a pretext for war. On Christmas 1862 a corps commanded by Brigadier General Sherman was pushing toward Vicksburg, Mississippi, but the costly siege of the river fortress would end only on July 4, 1863, as the carnage at Gettysburg continued. On Christmas 1863 a Federal force bombarded and took St. John's Island, off South Carolina, to impede the blockade running that supplied the South while shipping off its cotton to raise desperately needed revenue and buy munitions. The capture of Vicksburg in July had cut the Confederacy in two, and the simultaneous failure by Lee at Gettysburg had put victory beyond reach. Sherman's cutting the viable remainder in two at Savannah by Christmas 1864 ended any chances for the South's survival.

Although Savannah was offered dramatically—yet almost accidentally—as Lincoln's Christmas gift, the president's more significant geographical present had come earlier. That was Atlanta. His political survival and the future of the rebellion turned on it. Had Sherman been thwarted at Atlanta, especially at an agonizing price, the likely dismay of the press and the public in the North, and the reversal in the Federal bayonet vote in the South, would have been enormous. The peace ticket might have then prevailed and the crucial Savannah campaign been aborted. Abraham Lincoln would have returned home to his law practice in Springfield, Illinois. President-elect George Brinton McClellan would have been inaugurated on March 4, 1865, five weeks before Lincoln, reelected, sat in the presidential box at Ford's Theatre watching *Our American Cousin* while John Wilkes Booth, a celebrated actor and fanatical secessionist known to the backstage crew, slipped in to alter the peace although not the war.

The city by the sea would have remained—until slavery slowly eroded through other means—its leisurely antebellum self, with its elegant homes, squares, and society—thriving, thanks to a submissive, exploited, slave underclass. Even so, Savannah's evacuation and surrender saved it from the firestorm of Atlanta.

Atlanta made Savannah possible—a Christmas gift not merely for Lincoln, but for the Union. For the Confederacy, survival for a few stubborn, desperate, costly further months was all that remained. Had peace come sooner after Savannah, the vindictive swath of bummers and burning through the Carolinas would not have happened. War, especially unwinnable war, is the worst of political solutions.

SOURCES

Preface

Henry Clay Work's "Marching through Georgia" was published as sheet music by Root & Cady of Chicago in 1865. Sherman's letter to the minister missing his horse, September 16, 1864, is reprinted from the *New Hampshire Statesman*, May 26, 1865. For other Sherman letters, see notes to chapter 1, below.

1.
Voting with Their Feet

News reported in the press is cited throughout the text by newspaper title, or, if published widespread, without identifying a particular paper. The *Savannah News* is quoted from the *Mobile Daily Advertiser and Register*, February 4, 1864, in Larry E. Nelson's *Bullets, Ballots, and Rhetoric: Confederate Policy for the United States Presidential Contest of 1864* (University: University of Alabama Press, 1980). This source misspells *internecine*; it is corrected here.

For Thanksgiving, North and South, see James S. Robbins, "Giving Thanks in Wartime: The Soldiers' and Sailors' Thanksgiving of 1864," *National Review Online*, November 24, 2004. Charles A. Dana's coordination of the Union Thanksgiving in the field is in his *Recollections of the Civil War* (New York: D. Appleton, 1898). Georgia newspapers belittling Union soldiery early in the war, and even before the war, are quoted in James M. McPherson, *Battle Cry of Freedom: The Civil War Era* (New York: Oxford University Press, 1988). McPherson is also the source for Lee's joking Christmas letter, quoted in his article "Götterdämmerung," *The New York Review of Books*, December 21, 1995, p. 15. General Sherman's memoirs (orig. 1875, 1886) are from the text in *Memoirs of General W. T. Sherman* (New York: Library of America, 1990).

For the soldier vote, the most complete source beyond press accounts, including remarks by Lincoln and Grant, is Josiah Henry Benton, *Voting in the Field: A Forgotten Chapter of the Civil War* (Boston: privately printed, 1915). For the peace ticket, see Jennifer L. Weber, *Copperheads: The Rise and Fall of Lincoln's Opponents in the North* (New York: Oxford University Press, 2006). Unless otherwise noted here or in the text, soldier comments on the balloting are from these sources, quoting home letters and diaries. The Copperhead-Union dialogue is reported in the *Portsmouth Journal* of New Hampshire, September 17, 1864. General Hooker's impromptu political speech is reported in the *Portsmouth Morning Chronicle*, also of New Hampshire, September 13, 1864. John Jones's Richmond diary is quoted in Anne J. Bailey, *The Chessboard of War: Sherman and Hood in the Autumn Campaigns of 1864* (Lincoln: University of Nebraska Press, 2000). Lincoln's memorandum to his cabinet is reported in David Herbert Donald's *Lincoln* (New York: Doubleday, 1995). Thurlow Weed's melancholy prediction is quoted by Stephen W. Sears in *George B. McClellan: The Young Napoleon* (New York: Ticknor & Fields, 1988).

Sherman's letters throughout are from his memoirs and from *Sherman's Civil War: Selected Correspondence, 1860–1865* (Chapel Hill: University of North Carolina Press, 1999), eds. Brooks D. Simpson and Jean V. Berlin. (These include his *Home Letters* from the war, originally published in 1909.) Grant on Sherman's "boning" is quoted in many sources, here from Jim Miles's *To the Sea: A History and Tour Guide of Sherman's March* (Nashville: Rutledge Hill Press, 1989). Henry Hitchcock's letters and campaign diaries were published as *Marching with Sherman*, ed. Mark DeWolfe Howe (New Haven: Yale University Press, 1927). Theodore Upson's diary is *With Sherman to the Sea*, ed. O. O. Winther (Baton Rouge: Louisiana State University Press, 1943). Mary Boykin Chesnut's *A Diary from Dixie* (New York: D. Appleton, 1905), very likely accurate in details, was nevertheless expanded from memory after the war. *The Diary of Dolly Lunt Burge, 1848–1879* is edited by Christine Jacobson Garner (Athens: University of Georgia Press, 1997).

Private Francis R. Baker's diary is SC 69 in the Abraham Lincoln Presidential Library, Springfield, Illinois. Private Taylor's letters are in *Tom Taylor's Civil War* (Lawrence: University Press of Kansas, 2000). Major Thomas Ward Osborn is quoted from his *The Fiery Trail: A Union Officer's Account of Sherman's Last Campaigns*, eds. Richard Harwell and Philip N. Racine (Knoxville: University of Tennessee Press, 1986). Private Grant Taylor's correspondence with his wife, here and later, is from *This Cruel War: The Civil War Letters of Grant and Malinda Taylor, 1862–1865*, eds., Ann K. Blomquist and Robert A. Taylor (Macon, GA: Mercer University Press, 2000). The disproportionate Confederate casualties, given the South's smaller population, are estimated in Chandra Manning, *What This Cruel War Was Over: Soldiers, Slavery, and the Civil War* (New York: Knopf, 2008). Commander Craven is quoted from the *Portsmouth Daily Chronicle* of New Hampshire, December 20, 1864.

2.
Marching from Atlanta

Details of both wings of the march from Atlanta first appeared in Col. S. M. Bowman and Lt. Col. R. B. Irwin, *Sherman and His Campaigns: A Military Biography* (New York: Charles B. Richardson, 1865). Dozens of later accounts other than first-person narratives appear to be drawn from it. Rice Bull is quoted from *Soldiering: The Civil War Diary of Rice C. Bull*, ed. K. Jack Bauer (Novato, Calif.: Presidio Press, 1977). Hitchcock here and later is quoted from his diary, above. Jeff Davis was quoted often in the contemporary press, North and South, usually from newspapers in Richmond. The Tennessean postponing Christmas into January is quoted from material in the Texas Historical Center, Austin, in Penne L. Restad, *Christmas in America: A History* (New York: Oxford University Press, 1995).

For Sherman's correspondence here and later, see above. Private Upson is quoted above. For Dana, see above. Charles W. Wills's diaries and letters, portions of which were originally in *United States Service Magazine*, 1865, are collected in *Army Life of an Illinois Soldier* (Washington, D.C.: Globe, 1906). O. O. Howard's memoir is the *Autobiography of Oliver Otis Howard* (New York: Baker & Taylor, 1907). Sherman's field orders and his prewar personal history are from his memoirs.

The Shady Dale episode was described somewhat differently by a general and by a soldier in the ranks. General Carlin's "The March to the Sea: an Armed Picnic" first appeared in the June 11 and June 18, 1885, issues of the *National Tribune* as part of his serialized military memoirs. Michael Dresbach's account to his wife, December 14, 1864, in the Minnesota Historical Society Archives, is quoted by Bell Irvin Wiley in *The Life of Billy Yank: The Common Soldier of the Union* (Baton Rouge: Louisiana State University Press, 1978). "Geechee" dialect and slave music are described by Jacqueline Jones in *Saving Savannah: The City and the Civil War* (New York: Knopf, 2008), hereafter noted briefly as *Saving Savannah*.

For Mary Chesnut's diaries, see note to chapter 1. Mrs. Edmondston's diaries are collected in *Journal of a Secesh Lady: The Diary of Catherine Ann Devereux Edmondston*, ed. Beth G. Crabtree and James W. Patton (Raleigh, N.C.: Division of Archives and History, 1979).

3.
The Long Picnic

Emma High of Madison, A. C. Cooper of Eatonton, and Louise Cornwell of Hillsborough are quoted in Katherine M. Jones, *When Sherman Came: Southern Women and the "Great March"* (Indianapolis: Bobbs-Merrill, 1964). Corydon Foote here and later is quoted from his *With Sherman to the Sea: A Drummer's Story of the Civil War, as Related by Corydon Edward Foote to Olive Deane Hormel* (New York: John Day, 1960). For Dolly Burge, see above, chapter 1. Frederick Price and John Fuller are quoted in Burke Davis, *Sherman's March* (New York: Random House, 1980). "Bertha's" letter on Wheeler's depredations was quoted in *Countryman* in January 1865. Frederick Buerstatte's diary (in German) as translated by George Erme is in Special Collections, Carl Vinson Institute of Government, University of Georgia; presented by the Digital Library of Georgia. Enoch Weiss is quoted from Steven E. Woodworth, *Nothing but Victory: The Army of the Tennessee* (New York: Knopf, 2005). Major Capers is quoted from his report to Henry C. Wayne in the *Oxford Dictionary of Civil War Quotations*, ed. John D. Wright (New York, Oxford University Press, 2006).

For the Kentucky Rebels, see William C. Davis, *The Orphan Brigade: The Kentucky Confederates Who Couldn't Go Home* (Garden City, N.Y.: Doubleday, 1980). For Richard Taylor at Macon, see Taylor's *Destruction and Reconstruction: Personal Experiences of the Late War* (New York: Appleton, 1879). Mrs. Godkins of Hillsborough is quoted in the *Concord* (New Hampshire) *Monitor*, December 30, 1864, from the *Cincinnati Commercial*. For Charles Wills here and later, see chapter 1, above. Sherman's wry suggestion that chickens "roost very high" was reported in the *Portsmouth Daily Gazette* of New Hampshire, March 15, 1865. The summary of press comments on where Sherman was going are from John F. Marszalek, *Sherman's Other War: The General and the Civil War Press* (Kent, Ohio: Kent State University Press, 1999).

4.
Making Georgia Howl

For Anna Maria Green and A. C. Coooper, see *When Sherman Came*, above, chapter 3. E. D. Westfall is quoted in J. Cutler Andrews, ed., *The North Reports the Civil War* (Pittsburgh: University of Pittsburgh Press, 1955). The geography of Milledgeville circa 1864 and the account of the local schoolboy militia are from James C. Bonner, *Milledgeville: Georgia's Antebellum Capital* (Athens: University of Georgia Press, 1978). John Chipman Gray is quoted from *War Letters: 1862–1865*, eds. John Chipman Gray and John Codman Ropes (Boston: Houghton Mifflin, 1927).

The report of bloodhound abuse of Crummel, Harris, and Clors is from the *Cincinnati Gazette*. The allegation of the surgeon of the 14th Wisconsin about the mass slaughter of bloodhounds is reported in William Lloyd Garrison's newspaper *The Liberator,* January 27, 1865. For Rice Bull here and later, see chapter 2, above. Major James A. Connolly's memoir is *Three Years in the Army of the Cumberland,* ed. Paul Angle (Bloomington: Indiana University Press, 1959, 1987). Private Amos Stearns's Thanksgiving at Andersonville Prison is reported from *The Civil War Diary of Amos Stearns,* ed. Leon Basile (Rutherford, N.J.: Farleigh Dickinson University Press, 1981).

Alexander Collie's offer of cotton profits to Milledgeville relief is from Brian Jenkins, *Britain and the War for the Union, II* (Montreal: McGill–Queen's University Press, 1980). Dayton, the old lady, and her spinster daughter are reported by Hitchcock, above, as are the accounts of Mrs. Green and Kilpatrick's gross weeding out of his weakest horses. For Richard Taylor with Hardee in Savannah, see Taylor, above, chapter 3. Further press accounts speculating on Sherman's future direction are from J. Cutler Andrews, *The South Reports the Civil War* (Princeton: Princeton University Press, 1970).

5.
Left Wing/Right Wing

The correspondence between the Taylors here and later is *This Cruel War: The Civil War Letters of Grant and Malinda Taylor,* eds. Ann K. Blomquist and Robert A.

Taylor (Macon, Ga.: Mercer University Press, 2000). The facetious foraging "rules" by a private in the 113th Ohio are quoted by Joseph T. Glatthaar in *The March to the Sea and Beyond: Sherman's Troops in the Savannah and Carolina Campaigns* (New York: New York University Press, 1985). For Major Connolly, see above, chapter 4. Captain Charles Belknap's memoir about rescuing the abandoned girls is "Recollections of a Bummer," *The War of the Sixties,* ed. Edward R. Hutchins (New York: Neale, 1912). Belknap's earlier rescuing adventure in Roswell is documented in the collections of the Grand Rapids, Michigan, Public Library (courtesy of Ruth Van Stee, February 26, 2008).

For "Fighting Joe" Wheeler's harassment of the Federals amid the decline of Confederate fortunes, see Edward G. Longacre, *A Soldier to the Last: Maj. Gen. Joseph Wheeler in Blue and Gray* (Washington, D.C.: Potomac Books, 2007). For Tom Osborn, formerly a major, see chapter 1, above. For General Carlin, see above, chapter 2. Nora M. Canning's recollection of Kilpatrick's bummers, published in 1889, is reprinted in *When Sherman Came,* chapter 3, above. Herschel V. Johnson's visit by bummers was reported in the Northern press in January 1865. For Mary A. H. Gay, see her *Life in Dixie During the War: 1861–1865* (Atlanta, Ga.: Foote & Davies, 1894). Dr. Richard Arnold's proclamation as Savannah mayor calling citizens to arms was published in the local press on November 28 and thereafter in newspapers South and North. Sue Sample's reminiscence was reprinted in *When Sherman Came.* Northern reporters' conversations with "an old man named Wells" on November 29, 1864, reached the Northern press, including the *New York Evening Post,* by December 24. Major George W. Nichols's account is *The Story of the Great March: From the Diary of a Staff Officer* (New York: Harper & Brothers, 1865).

6.
". . . Just Like a Dose of Salts"

The "dose of salts" soldier verse is quoted in Glatthaar, above, chapter 5. For Connolly, see above, chapter 4. The "Blue Juniata" episode is described by the reporter from the *New York World* and by Hitchcock. The bathing soldiers episode is from the *World.* General Corse's signal to Sherman about being wounded is quoted by Sherman in his *Memoirs.*

The Rev. Emanuel Heidt's identity is confirmed by Chris Haynes of the United Methodist General Commission on Archives and History. Special Field Order No.

119, authorizing the holding back of "non-combatants" encumbering the march is in Sherman's memoirs. The numbers of slaves left behind and/or drowned at Ebenezer Creek vary from account to account, depending upon the emotions of the onlookers, but it is likely to have been in the low hundreds. Gen. Halleck's letter, citing the high end of estimates, is in Sherman's war letters. The "feeling of hardness" is quoted in Glatthaar, above, chapter 5. The *Savannah Morning News* of December 10, and Mayor Arnold's shipping his precious wines to safety, are from *Saving Savannah* (see notes to chapter 2).

For Private Taylor and Malinda see *This Cruel War*, above, chapter 5. The Griswoldville skirmish is recalled by Upson, Wills, and press accounts. Hitchcock's diary refers to the buried "torpedoes" and Sherman's response. Private Isaac Hermann (later a captain) published his recollections in *Memoirs of a Veteran Who Served as a Private in the 60's in the War between the States* (Lakemont, Ga: CSA Press, 1974, repr.). The memories of Laura Buttolph and Mary Jones Mallard are reprinted in *Yankees A'coming: One Month's Experience During the Invasion of Liberty County, Georgia, 1864–1865*, ed. Haskell Monroe (Tuscaloosa: Confederate Pub. Co., 1959). Mary Boykin Chesnut's diary recollections are from *A Diary from Dixie* (see notes to chapter 1).

For Private Buerstatte's diary, see chapter 3, above. Private Peters's diary is in Special Collections, SC 2407, Abraham Lincoln Presidential Library, Springfield, Ill. For Major Nichols, see above, chapter 5. General Howard's report of the Duncan scouting voyage is in his *Autobiography*, above, chapter 2.

7.
Besieging Savannah

For Duncan, see above, and the Northern press. For General Taylor and Mary Chesnut on General Lovell, see above. Captain Fox's report of hearing the bells of Savannah is from a letter to his father, the Rev. Thomas B. Fox, December 14, 1864, in the Fox Family Papers of the Massachusetts Historical Society, quoted by Michael Golay in *A Ruined Land: The End of the Civil War* (New York: Wiley, 1999). For descriptions, with illustrations, of the Confederate warships in Savannah harbor see *Civil War Naval Chronology: 1861–1865* (Washington, D.C.: Naval History Division, Navy Department, 1971, repr.). The attack on Fort McAllister is described by Hitchcock, Sherman, Howard, Nichols, and the Northern press. The most complete account of the exchange of flag signals before the attack, foreshortened in most accounts, is in Edward S. Cooper, *William Babcock Hazen: The Best Hated Man* (Madison, N.J.: Farleigh Dickinson University Press, 2005). For Major Osborn see chapter 1, above. The Grant-Sherman correspondence is in Sherman's memoirs and *The Papers of Ulysses S. Grant*, vol. 13, ed. John Y. Simon (Carbondale: Southern Illinois University Press, 1985). Sherman's failed ultimatum to Hardee and Hardeee's rejection are also in Sherman's memoirs. General Geary's letter to Mary Geary, Dec. 16, 1864, is in *A Politician Goes to War: The Civil War Letters of John White Geary*, ed. W. A. Blair (University Park: Pennsylvania State University Press, 1995). For Private Upson, see above.

Eliza Frances Andrews writes about her escape to Rebel territory in *The War-Time Journal of a Georgia Girl: 1864–1865* (New York: Appleton, 1908). Joseph LeConte's memoir is *'Ware Sherman: A Journal of Three Months' Personal Experience in the Last Days of the Confederacy* (Berkeley: University of California Press, 1937), largely drawn by his daughter Caroline from LeConte's *Autobiography* (New York: Appleton, 1903).

Frederick Price's letter to his wife, December 18, 1864, is quoted in Jim Miles's *To the Sea*, above, chapter 1. Henry Lea Graves's letter to his mother, and his brother Iverson's diary entry about the CSS *Georgia*, appear in footnotes in Glatthaar, above. The explosion of the *Georgia* is described by John Chipman Gray (above, chapter 4) to his mother in a letter on Christmas Day. For Private Upson and Major Nichols, see above. A good description of the building of the pontoon-and-rice flat bridge, drawn from Charles C. Jones's *The Siege of Savannah* (1874), is in Jack H. Lepa, *Breaking the Confederacy: The Georgia and Tennessee Campaigns of 1864* (Jefferson, N.C.: McFarland, 2005).

Albert Gallatin Browne's papers, including cotton vouchers, are at the Massachusetts Historical Society. Additional Browne papers are at Radcliffe College. The Sherman-Lincoln "Christmas gift" correspondence suggested by Browne is in Sherman's memoirs, but appeared earlier in the Northern press and Horace Greeley's book *The American Conflict. A History of the Great Rebellion in the United States of America, 1860–64, II* (Hartford, Conn.: O. D. Case, 1866).

8.
Savannah Christmas

Lincoln's letter to Sherman, reprinted in his *Memoirs*, was widely published in the daily press. The 200-gun salute in Washington was reported by the Associated Press.

The casualty totals for the march are cited in *Sherman and His Campaigns*, above, chapter 2. The attack on Fort Fisher is from Don Lowry, *Towards an Indefinite Shore: The Final Months of the Civil War* (New York: Hippocrene, 1995), and Robert E. Denney, *The Civil War Years: A Day-by-Day Chronicle* (New York: Gramercy, 1992). Fred Grant's visit is in Grant's *Papers*, above, chapter 7. The plea to Sherman about care of Rebel general spouses is in his memoirs and letters.

The British consul's dialogue with Sherman over warehoused cotton is conflated from an unidentified "Port Royal letter" of January 28, 1865, in the *Exeter News-Letter* of New Hampshire, February 13, 1865, and a dispatch attributed to the "Washington Correspondent of N. Y. Herald" in the *Portsmouth Journal of Literature and Politics*, April 8, 1865. Wimer Bedford's recollection of what happened to other valuables stored in the Molyneux mansion is in *Nothing but Victory*, above, chapter 3, drawn from the Bedford Papers in the Library of Congress. The Blakely guns from England are described by Osborn, above, chapter 1.

The anonymous Northern lady in Savannah writing about her Christmas dinner is quoted at length in "Unionists at Savannah," *Boston Evening Transcript*, January 14, 1865. For the Andrews sisters' journey, continued here, see Eliza's *War-Time Journal*, above, chapter 7. Frances Thomas Howard is quoted from *When Sherman Came*, above, chapter 3. "Fanny Cohen's Journal of Sherman's Occupation of Savannah," ed. Spencer B. King, Jr., from the Phillips-Myers Papers in the Southern Historical Collection, University of North Carolina at Chapel Hill, is in *The Georgia Historical Quarterly*, XLI, 4 (December 1957). The *Savannah Loyal Georgian* is quoted from the December 26, 1864, issue, described as volume 1, no. 2.

The Minnesota private at church is quoted from Jesse Bean's diary in the Jesse Bean Papers, SRC (above), in Glatthaar. Sherman's rejoinder to a clergyman ostensibly permitting him to pray for Jeff Davis and the Devil is in a letter to Mary Geary from her husband in his *Civil War Letters* (see chapter 7). The dialogue was quoted somewhat differently in the Northern press, but Geary was on the scene.

Private Buerstatte's Christmas tree at his tent is from his diary, chapter 3, above. Thomas Maguire's slaveowning Christmas is from Samuel Carter III, *The Siege of Atlanta, 1864* (New York: St. Martin's Press, 1973). The Christmas of Mary Sharpe Jones and Mary Jones Mallard is described in their *Yankees A'coming*, above, chapter 6. LeConte's adventures are continued from his *'Ware Sherman*, above, chapter 7. For the Orphan Brigade, see above, chapter 3.

For Captain Belknap and the children he had rescued, see Belknap, above, chapter 5. James Sawyer is quoted on Christmas Day to "Nancy" in Glatthaar, above, chapter 5. John Peters is quoted from his diary, above, chapter 6. Olney Andrus and an unnamed New Jersey soldier are quoted from Bell Irvin Wiley, *Billy Yank*, above, chapter 2. For Amos Stearns, see chapter 4. The private willing to go hungry "somb times" and the description of provisions-laden wagons drawn by mules dressed as reindeer are from Glatthaar, above, chapter 5.

9.
Christmas Week in the Union

Geary's letter to his wife is in his *Civil War Letters,* above, chapter 7. Sherman's account of the early days in Savannah is from his memoirs. The orderly distribution of emergency food supplies is reported in the *Boston Evening Transcript*, January 30, 1865. The pleas from "venomous" Southern ladies at first rebuffed by General Blair are described in the *Portsmouth Daily Chronicle* of New Hampshire, February 25, 1865. For Fanny Cohen and Frances Howard, see above, chapter 8. General Howard's standoff with a Rebel lady is described in his autobiography and by Burke Davis, above, chapter 2. Howard describes his conversation with Sherman about a leave to see his children in his autobiography. For Nichols, see above, chapter 5.

For Private Jarrett and Chaplain Hight, see *Billy Yank*, above, chapter 2. For Private Peters, see his diary, above, chapter 6. For Private Stearns in Andersonville, see chapter 4. Charles Wills (above, chapter 1 and following) writes to his sister about the "sweetest girl" he has encountered in Savannah. For Richmond clerk John Jones, see his diary as quoted in *The Chessboard of War*, above, chapter 1. Captain Foster is quoted from Samuel T. Foster, *One of Cleburne's Command: The Civil War Reminiscences and Diary of Capt. Samuel T. Foster, Granbury's Texas Brigade, CSA,* ed. Norman D. Brown (Austin: University of Texas Press, 1980).

The capture of the blockade runner *Rebecca Hertz* is cited in *Boston Evening Transcript*, January 4, 1865, and in the Chatham County, Georgia, Archives, which identify the vessel. (Sherman refers to it vaguely in his memoirs.) For Mary Chesnut, Mary Mallard, and Joseph LeConte, see above. William Gilmore Simms is referred to in the *Portland* (Maine) *Transcript*, March 11, 1865. Sherman recalls his and Howard's visit to the Gordons in his memoirs; also in Burke Davis, above, drawn from Juliette Gordon Low's "When I Was a Girl," in Anne Hyde Choate and Helen Ferris, *Juliette Low and the Girl Scouts* (Garden City, N.Y.: Doubleday Doran, 1928). For Corydon Foote's memoir, see above, chapter 3.

The citizen queue for the amnesty oath was reported in the *Savannah Republi-*

can on December 31, 1864. The burial rites for infant Charles Sherman are drawn from the *New York Times,* December 25, 1864. The culminating parade of firemen and their equipages is described in the *Philadelphia Inquirer* in a dispatch dated December 31, 1864. The prewar composition of the fire department and its prewar annual parade in May are from *Saving Savannah* (notes, chapter 2).

The *Richmond Whig,* January 10, 1865, concedes "the most perfect order" in occupied Savannah. The citizens' meeting and its resolutions are from *The Liberator,* January 18, 1865. The unnamed "private citizen" writing from Savannah to his brother in the North on December 30, 1864, is quoted at length in the *Rochester Express* of New York State, reprinted in the *Boston Evening Transcript,* January 12, 1865.

ACKNOWLEDGMENTS

For their assistance in researching and creating *General Sherman's Christmas* I am indebted, beyond the sources above, to Robert C. Doyle, William F. Duncan, Elisabeth Dyssegaard, Victor Greto, Robert Guinsler, Chris Haynes, Carie Lee Kennedy, Michael Lipschutz, Timothy D. Murray, Michel Pharand, Warren C. Robinson, Cheryl Schnirring, Ruth Van Stee, Mark B. Weintraub, Rodelle Weintraub, and Richard E. Winslow.

INDEX